ACCLAIM FOR CAROLYN SEE AND *GOLDEN DAYS*

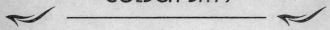

"THERE IS SOMETHING ALMOST [HENRY] JAMESIAN ABOUT SEE'S NOVEL ... A RICHLY INTELLIGENT, CULTURALLY DISCERNING NOVEL."

CHICAGO TRIBUNE

"SEE'S DESCRIPTIONS OF THE PHYSICAL WORLD ARE VIVID, SOMETIMES MOVING.... GOLDEN DAYS IS FILLED WITH QUIRKY AND QUITE REALISTIC CHARACTERS."

NEWSDAY

"CAROLYN SEE MAKES YOU BOTH PROUD TO BE A WOMAN AND A LITTLE SCARED TO BE A MAN. BUT SHE DOES THIS WITH THE WIT AND RESOURCEFULNESS ONE HAS GOT USED TO AS A READER, AND VICTIM, OF HER BOOK REVIEWS. SHE HAS A PENETRATING EYE AND (DARE I SAY?) A MOTHERLY ATTITUDE TOWARD A WORLD WHOSE CONFUSIONS MARVELOUSLY IRRITATE HER, AND, THROUGH HER, AMUSE US."

WILLIAM F. BUCKLEY, JR.

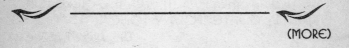

(MORE)

"*GOLDEN DAYS* OFFERS THE EXCITEMENT OF DISCOVERING WHAT SEEMS LIKE A BRAND-NEW TALENT, BUT ENRICHED BY A SURENESS OF TRAGICOMIC TOUCH THAT COULD ONLY BE THE WORK OF AN EXPERIENCED WRITER STRIKING INTO BOLD NEW TERRITORY."

PUBLISHERS WEEKLY

"A WONDERFUL BOOK. TO READ IT IS TO GO BEYOND DENIAL OF THE UNTHINKABLE TO SOME CRAZY HOPE. IF SUCH A HEROINE CAN BE SO TRULY IMAGINED HERE AND NOW, SHE MIGHT EMBOLDEN US TO SAVE OURSELVES. I SALUTE HER."

BETTY FRIEDAN,
AUTHOR OF *THE FEMININE MYSTIQUE*

"THE STYLE IS ENERGETIC, ALMOST AS IF SEE WERE WRITING ON ROLLER SKATES.... HER WRITING IS FIRMLY ROOTED IN SOUTHERN CALIFORNIA...."

MINNEAPOLIS STAR & TRIBUNE

"AMUSING, MANIC ... SHE HAS A SHARP SATIRICAL TALENT AND SHE PUTS IT TO USE HERE ON A STRIKINGLY CONTEMPORARY TOPIC."

THE KIRKUS REVIEWS

GOLDEN DAYS

CAROLYN SEE

FAWCETT CREST • NEW YORK

To John Espey,
with love,

and to the
Boy Who Could Melt
Through Walls

A Fawcett Crest Book
Published by Ballantine Books
Copyright © 1987 by Carolyn See

Library of Congress Catalog Number: 86-2830

ISBN 0-449-21437-0

This edition published by arrangement with McGraw-Hill, Inc.

Manufactured in the United States of America

First Ballantine Books Edition: December 1987

Sitting in the park in Paris, France
Reading the news, and it sure looks bad.
They won't give peace a chance
That was just a dream some of us had . . .

Ah, but California,
California, I'm coming home.
I'm gonna see the folks I dig,
I'll even kiss the Sunset pig,
California, I'm coming home.

—Joni Mitchell

                              Mean while
The world shall burn, and from her ashes spring
New heaven and earth, wherein the just shall dwell,
And after all their tribulations long
See golden days, fruitful of golden deeds,
With joy and love triumphing, and fair truth.

—*Paradise Lost*, Book III

PART 1

APRIL-NOVEMBER 1980

ONCE, I REMEMBER, IN AN ENTIRELY DIFFERENT WORLD, I interviewed that East Coast photographer who made a good living taking pictures of people as they jumped. He asked if he could take a picture of me, and I jumped! I put everything into it! I took a look outside of his white studio into the grimy New York streets below; I thought of how I'd jumped from a ratty house with a tired mom, past two husbands, one sad, one mad; hopscotched with kids and lovers and ended up—here? In *New York*! I sized up the directions of the room, tried to find east. I started out from there, ran a maximum of ten heavy steps, and jumped—not far, not far enough by a long shot—and came down hard.

The photographer winced. "Try it again," he said.

So I went back to the far corner, ran, defied gravity, jumped. This time I held up my arms, held up my chin, grinned. His camera clicked. "That's it."

"*That's it*?"

"You only have one jump in you," he said. (I found out later he said it to everybody.)

That wasn't fair. But maybe it was right. I began to notice —I date it from that day, not that it was new material—most of us have just one story in us; we live it and

3

breathe it and think it and go to it and from it and dance with it; we lie down with it, love it, hate it, and that's our story.

About that time I noticed something else: There was a ratio involved here. Just as those poor woolly headed American nigras only got seven-tenths of the vote (after the Civil War, if and when they *got* the vote—I can't really remember), so, too, there was a basic inequality in the country I grew up in and lived in. One man, one story. For women, it generally took two or even three to make one story. So that in shopping malls you sometimes saw two fat women waddling along, casting sidelong glances at one another's fat. Or two pretty girls outprettying each other. Two femmes fatales, eyeing each other's seductions.

This is partly the story of Lorna Villanelle and me; two ladies absolutely crazed with the secret thought that they were something special. But if you think you aren't going to care about this story, hold on. It's the most important story in the Western world!

Believe me.

Take this for a story. It's four in the afternoon: 1950 something. A chunky thirteen-year-old walks home after school, kicking at leaves with heavy shoes, up the buckling sidewalks of Micheltorena Hill, in the parched and arid heart of Los Angeles. She dawdles, she doesn't want to get there. Her father's gone, there's no joy here now, or ever, maybe. At 3:45 she drifts down through a small "Spanish" patio and into a house that perches precariously on the side of this hill—crackling with dried and golden rye grass—bangs the door, clumps down the tiled hall to the sunken living room, where she sees her mother crying. Her mother looks up, twists her tear-stained linen handkerchief, and says, with all the vindictiveness a truly heartbroken woman can muster, "*Must you always be so heavy?*"

The thirteen-year-old, her face flushed from the sun, the

walk, and pure shame, walks on tiptoe without speaking, past her mother to the picture window, which faces diagonally west. She doesn't think to look below, to the patio perfect for parties they'll never give, but only *out*, out to the horizon where, past twenty miles of miniature city, the ocean—thin strip—catches the afternoon sun, and blazes. Ah!

"*Don't* put your head on the window!" her mother snaps, and the girl lurches back as if the window burned, but her forehead mark, brain fingerprint, remains.

AFTER THE DAY OF THE CLUMSY JUMP I REALIZED I WASN'T built to live in New York. It was the greatest city in the world, but I couldn't get on its pretty side. I'll go further and say that after several short trips to Paris, Madrid, Rome, I realized that I'd been going in the wrong direction; the further east you got the further back *in* you were. By now I could look at my life as a series of sterling wrong choices: a marriage to an exquisitely handsome artist that had yielded up nothing more than a princess of a daughter, beautiful as the dawn—hence her fancy name, Aurora— and another marriage to an Australian on the make, who'd seen *me* as a meal ticket (poor deluded mate!), and that marriage had given me an emerald tomboy. Her dad, Dirk Langley (his name eventually to be spelled—incorrectly— on theater marquees in both hemispheres), wanted to call our baby "Denny," but I'd insisted on the sleepy and elegant French, Denise. . . . I'd majored in the wrong things in college, lived precariously in Manhattan's wrong sections. Now I wanted, so much, more than I can say, to get out.

And so, at the age of thirty-eight, I came back to L.A., I came back. I would live a gentle mimicry of my mother's story, alone with my two girls. I planned to earn my own money, and never to cry, and never to lay about with the cruel weapons of spite. I would take accounting courses. I would become a person who knew about riches, so that when people heard my name (when I became famous) they wouldn't hear "Edith Langley," who made two bad marriages and had to make her own way (or even, isn't she the *heavy* one who made the house shake when she came home from school?), but Edith Langley, whose name meant money, and money meant power.

Los Angeles, in 1980, was a different city from the one I'd left. I drove far out, to Santa Monica, found a bad motel, with two double beds and a television that worked. Then, after a day or two, I put Aurora and Denise in the back seat of the old Porsche and went house hunting.

I drove with the kids one dreadful morning into the San Fernando Valley and felt that if there had to be a nuclear war, certainly it might do some good in this area. I drove through Topanga Canyon, fifteen miles from the Valley to the coast (like Switzerland after the A-bomb, some friend of mine had said years before), hands sweating on the steering wheel as I took the curves, and had to think that maybe I wasn't ready for the Canyon; maybe I just didn't have the nerve. I braked at the Pacific, knowing that Malibu was north and no way could I afford it yet. I turned south, looking for Venice . . . and headed—like a gerbil in a cage—back downtown.

They say L.A. is large, but they lie. It's true there are a zillion places no one in his right mind would like: Lakewood, Torrance, Brea, Compton, Carson, no one *real* lived there, any more than real people lived in those grey asphalt boxes that line the roads between New York's airport and its island. "Real" L.A. had its thick, coiled root downtown, and on the east, little underground rootlets; obscure Mexican restaurants. Then a thin stem, the Santa Monica freeway, heading due west and putting out greenery, places in this western desert where you'd love to live— if things went right.

I headed west again: Echo Park, old houses, fine artists in them. I didn't like the neighborhood; it was too close to where I'd started. Further west and to the right, the Hollywood Hills with the sign and all, and Aldous Huxley's widow tucked in just below the H. The *air* was still too thick for me. Sixty miles an hour and ten minutes later, there was Westwood to look at. A pretty town, safe, and rich, and if the kids wanted to go to UCLA, perfect for them. But the rents started at $800.

Hard to please? Got it from my mom. A charmer? Well, three lone souls out of four million might agree. I wanted the beach, so bad. I got back on the stem, ever closer to the great Pacific. So! North along the coast again, just for the ride, and something made me turn in again at steep, sparsely populated Topanga Canyon.

It was late in the day, maybe four o'clock, on an April afternoon. I'd driven through eastern sleet to get here, and "unseasonal" snow in the Rockies, and heat like a flat plate in the High Desert. But here, it was . . . perfect. April is the time for ceanothus in the Canyon and great banks of bright blue I'd find out later were lupin. There was even, if you can believe it, a waterfall, a long silver string dropping casually off a high stone abutment. The trip inland started out shallow, against low hills. After a half-dozen tricky twists and turns we hit a half-mile straightaway, starting at the bottom of what seemed (that first time) like a thousand-foot-high cliff, and climbed steadily, hugging the northwest side of the canyon wall. My hands started sweating, slick on the wheel, and Aurora, my older daughter, lay down in back. "Tell me when it's over," she whispered.

But I've thought many times that, though I'd taken those early curves at a cautious twenty-five miles an hour, I resisted *even then* the temptation to speed up on the straightaway between the coast and the town, that piece of bad driving that forever separates the Canyon from the city dweller.

At the top of that half-mile run (which, I found out later, had to be rebuilt every five years as the rains washed it out) the road curled into three or four really spellbinding curves: How easy, I thought even then, to keep going straight when the road turned left, to arc out into *nothing* for one last carnival ride.

Ten minutes later I drew up, trembling, to a small stone building. We were in mountain country, for sure. Was this what I'd been looking for as I pressed my damp head against my mother's polished picture window? Do you think—*might* I have seen these fragrant cliffs from there?

"I'm going to throw up," Denise, my younger one, said. "I mean it. And I'm hungry!"

We stopped at a place called the Discovery Inn (Innkeeper, Marge Dehr). The inside smelled of dried flowers and old hamburger.

"What do *you* want?"

"Are you the hostess?"

"What if I am?"

"Could we . . ."

I remember myself: tired, rasping voice, dirt brown hair frizzed out like that black woman's whose name I forget, my first diamonds—three-quarters of a carat (bought at what price!) jammed in my ears, eyeliner, dirt under my nails.

"We need a place to live."

"Don't you think it's a little fucking *late in the day*?"

"I thought . . ." I didn't know what I thought. "I just want to be sure that I get the kids back down before it gets dark . . ."

"The *kids* don't care! Sit down and eat. Order a Swinger. They're the best. Anyway, if you can't get *down* out of here, there's no point in coming *up*."

I couldn't argue with this logic. We ate, then groped

our way back down the mountain to our crummy motel room. I watched the girls' faces as they watched television in one double bed; it's clear, or should be, that they were dearer to me than five hundred crates of diamond earrings in five hundred solid gold pick-up trucks.

The next morning we drove back up—those curves almost a snap by now—loving that pure *climb* into the sky and the feeling that once you got up there, in those mountains north of Santa Monica, you were safe; they couldn't get to you. (And later I learned that during Prohibition outlaws from all over California vamoosed to Topanga, because all the overlapping city limits that made up Los Angeles had left one lawless hole.)

In the cool morning air, with theatrical wisps of ground fog drifting up and over the harsh mountains from the Pacific, we rendezvoused at that ratty restaurant. Marge Dehr came slouching out, introduced us to a "realtor" who whisked up in a powder blue Ferrari. He drove us around all through the day, up one dizzying unpaved road after another. On one cliff you might see great grim stretches of that modern midden the San Fernando Valley, and on another rocky outcropping you might climb, creaking, out of that guy's cramped little cockroach of a car, walk ten steps down a dusty incline, and there see a sturdy *blue world*, a blue saddle shoe, light on top—that would be the sky —and on the bottom more dark blue than you could ever imagine in one place, the vast Pacific. Of course the houses with that dizzying prospect, mostly three-story, white stucco, and a million dollars apiece, were a little out of our range. But down in the strange dank hollows and washed-out deltas in the bowl of the canyon itself— an indentation of about five square miles, I'd guess, where clothing stores perched on creek banks and welfare mothers with sunny smiles watched their naked kids slushing in the mud—you could rent a trailer for thirty-five dollars a week.

As we drove, Aurora and Denise, usually impatient or droopy or long-suffering, began to get a dreamy look. The morning lengthened into hot, aromatic midday. "That's dodder, that orange stuff on the bushes," the house tout might say, and in the next breath he'd try out, "Of course a carpet like this is going to be unusual in the Canyon," or "You don't see a chandelier like this every day, up here." We even drove as far back west—down the canyon—to hit the "Gulch," a low, flat, damp place just across the highway from the ocean itself. Down in that low wash fifty people must have dumped their cars where the Topanga Creek seeped into swamp, and yards of trailing morning glories had turned each one of them into a blue mountain.

"D'rather go *up*," Denise said, slapping at mosquitoes.

"I think," I said to them, "I must have been to a party here once, years ago. I'm sure of it . . ."

But the man shrugged impatiently and, zipping us back up the steep slopes back to the dead center of this ever-better world, said, "Think we'll turn left into Old Canyon this time. Some people say this is the *tough* part. Some people say this is the *desert* part. Other people like it. I couldn't say." Then, glancing at me shrewdly as his jeweled and tan hands on the wheel expertly took these curves, shrouded on either side by beige stone and nothing else, "*This* road we're on is always the first to go out in winter when the rains come. Have to get out by horse through here. When the fires come, they take you out by helicopter. Most people stay though. Save their houses. Take a few trash cans, fill 'em with water, beat out the flames with rug scraps." Then, jerking his head, "Indians used to fish in the creek here. They used wild cucumber to float their nets . . ."

The house sat out on a wide raw crescent of cut and fill. That half-moon of dirt hung, just hung there in the air, over another one of those astonishing cliffs above nowhere. Across the chasm from what might be our "back-yard" were stones the size of skyscrapers. Due east, a wilderness of bougainvillea and eucalyptus, sage, rose-mary, mint, and a couple of blazing yellow acacias. We might have been in Australia with just a couple of aborig-ines for company, but instead we could hear Van Morri-son, the Doors, windchimes, barking dogs. We smelled marijuana with the rosemary, and the house tout said, siz-ing us up, "If this section of the canyon caught fire, the city'd be high for a week. They *say.*" And in the next breath talked about the wonderful elementary school.

Two stories, made out of fresh new cedar slats on the outside, California white-sheeted clapboard on the inside (no fireplace, a definite minus in the Canyon, where once every decade or so it had been known to snow great flakes), and all this only forty minutes away from down-town L.A.! There was no yard yet, this was a new place, just golden dust all around. Our neighbors "next door"— a shack a hundred yards up the grade—said later that we'd be living in rattlesnake heaven, but listen! Past where the bulldozers had rousted out those fiendish vipers, the *real* view started!

For years I had a picture of my daughters from that time, standing by a yucca taller than they were. They both had that dreamy look, the kind that used to make people in the city say that everybody up here was on drugs, but what it meant was that they were happy.

I'm not saying it was easy! God forbid. Do you think it's easy for a single mother who has "financial consult-ant" printed on her business cards to get credit in the greater Los Angeles area? My husbands found out I was back and put in some mean-spirited phone calls, the more so because I suggested they might like to kick in a little child support. And sweet spring rapidly turned into a sum-mer so outrageously *fucking hot* that by some paradox it turned the inside of our new house a luminous black. We'd already found that the lady in the restaurant owned this rickety house and paid Mr. Slicko in his ill-gotten car something like a thirty percent commission to get it off her hands.

There came a day in early September, down in the old market at the Center of the Canyon, where, barefoot, I stood in line, holding my brown rice and hamburger, dreaming New York dreams, thinking, Oh, God, *another* wrong turn? I'd already gained maybe thirty pounds from smoking the days away with those guys next door and then putting together vast casseroles liberally seasoned with all that indigenous fragrant stuff. I stood in the dark store, sweating, fretting as always, that half my life was over but really, all my life was over, I'd *had* it, when over by the antique gumball machine that stood by the rusting screen door—pushed out over many years by how many heedless customers—I heard and saw two filthy little boys scrambling against each other on the sticky cement floor. "It's mine, assbite motherfucker, I saw it first!" "Shit if it is, stupid shithead, I had it first and then I dropped it!"

Stolid and benumbed, I stood in line with other sweltering residents as the two kids gouged each other's noses and eyes, pulled hair, for what I sadly supposed would be a gumball. They dove together, under the machine, and each came up with one end of a very distressed snake, who, until that moment had probably thought of himself as no more than three feet long. For an eternal moment they hauled in some frantic tug-of-war with the snake, who said a silent snake-*awk*! Until the man behind the register said, "Get out of here with that, willya?" and they disappeared out into the 120-degree heat. A sigh from behind me. It came from an artist with a national reputation, wearing shoulder-length hair left over from the sixties, bald pate slick with sweat. "Kind of makes you wonder, doesn't it?"

Only two months later, when November turned the air

crisp, I was down in that same center, thin again, in a restaurant this time, drinking champagne for breakfast, picking at chicken livers and sour cream, when in this crowded, jovial, cozy place we heard a sound like a siren. A few of us went outside to see what was up, and there, in front of that same ratty grocery store, was a young man dressed all in white, doing a morning mantra. "Oooh," he sang, all on one note, "hooww beautiful is the Canyon in the morning!" He'd picked a note that made some of the parking-lot dogs crazy. One in particular danced about the guy, trying to put his paws around the singer's neck, howling happily on the same note. The singer had a girl-friend, or a devotée, who, since the singer definitely wasn't going either to stop or change his tune, undertook gently to shoo the dog back with a leafy branch. For minutes we stood out there, that Sunday morning, the breath coming in steam from our smiling mouths, watching boy, girl, and dog, hearing that song. Then went back in to finish break-fast.

If you think finding the right place just happens, you've got another think.

I BOUGHT AN ANSWERING MACHINE AND A REAM OF BUSI-ness stationery. And in a few weeks—after we'd settled in—I took another long L.A. drive. What I noticed—as they used to say on this coast—*what I noticed*, was that there were very few regular what you'd call *businesses*. No raincoat makers. No soup manufacturers. Yes, there were sweatshops in downtown L.A. and I remember a ceramics factory out in Glendale, but they soon went out of busi-ness. What was really out here was the *intangible*. When you drove you saw buildings, often windowless. They were either television stations or movie studios (or ingenious, semi-successful combinations of the two) or death factories where they made missiles, or think tanks where they

thought them up, or ingenious combinations of *those* two.
Who was I to give any of the people behind those walls
financial advice? I, who was thirty-eight years old and
divorced (twice!)? I ended up doing something, it seems
to me now, everyone in Los Angeles did then: I made
myself up half hour by hour. I rented myself out to silicone
chip places. I got myself a weekly financial column at the
city's "second" paper, which got me to parties, which got
me to cute guys, which got me to some financial meetings
of small businesses, and little by little I was able to build
up a fairly decent portfolio.

I changed my hairstyle, wore it straight to my shoulders,
frosted blond. I bought a new silk shirt a week. I knew
grey flannel was for New York only, but wouldn't raw silk
pass as the flannel of the desert? I began to buy, once
every month or so, another $500 suit, boxy tailored jacket,
soft skirt. I began to switch from pumps to expensive sandals. Some spring days I'd wear one bright hibiscus in my
hair.

But mostly, when I'd go out with some man who owned
yachts in the marina, or a cute ARCO executive, or that
lowest of the low out here, an "independent producer,"
he thinking he'd get a little free help in his wine futures,
I'd say, right up front, "Hey! you want advice? Don't think
your *dick* is going to pay me for it! I'll take semiprecious
stones. Or gold would be better!" Usually they were good
sports about it. I got some nice amethysts I *still* wear (and
I mean *now*) and pearls, of course, and finally those one
carat don't-fuck-me-over flawless diamonds that I stuck in
my ears and *never* took out—you'll notice, I still wear
them. My girls each kept one of that flawed but brave first
pair.

In the late seventies there was still a lot of personal
chaos around: I don't mean "love," I don't mean drugs.
I mean, when you got up in the morning it was hard to
know what style of underwear to put on, what style of

breakfast to eat. (Really!) Should it be ''nutritious'' the way that poor Adele Davis used to say? If so, why did she die so horribly of bone cancer, and why did it hurt so much? Should it be *quesadillas*? (A recent study had said coffee and cheese caused cancer.) Should it be fruit? (What about insecticide?)

When you went out with men in those days, young *or* old, married, single or divorced, there was a terrible help-lessness in them: What *next*, was in their every gesture, their every remark. Do we get married, or see a movie, or just have sex, or do errands? Are we supposed to be friends, or what is this *intimate* stuff they're talking about? Am I supposed to be cool? Do you want some cocaine? Do you like hockey? Do you want to meet my kids?

So you can see boxy jackets with loose skirts like the lady in the *Story of O*, and a forthright request for jewelry was a definite godsend for some of them.

I began to take my own advice. I diversified my invest-ments. I took a couple more extension courses at the great universities, and even then I began to see that, since the country itself was running at such a huge deficit, a single woman might easily make her mark in the world by stay-ing out of debt and building up a pound or so of rubies or a small safe deposit box of those sweet little gold ounce ingots from Macao, stamped with the sign of the bat—bad luck over here, but over there it meant long life and pros-perity.

Wealth! To me it began to seem like the only constant. Husbands and lovers came and went, and God love them! And sure, Aurora and Denise were my real wealth, but on the great conveyor belt of life, my children were sliding past me and away. Once I pushed rocks in my ears they were there forever. No one offered courses with that belief system at UCLA: no *stand firm*, keep the house in case of a divorce, avoid credit cards like the plague, hold that money close to your vest and buy *stones*. Finally, after about six months out here in this fairyland, my hometown, I took what seemed to me the quintessential L.A. step and began offering my own seminars. I took my jeweler's glass, or "diamond loupe," my briefcase, and two dozen good stones to an extension lady's home—out of UCLA, of course—and spoke to a class of affluent matrons. Ah, I *loved* it. I had a twentieth, a thirtieth, a fiftieth of what their husbands owned, my flimsy house in the Canyon was at the whim of any hot breeze or carelessly struck match. They lived in brick and stucco palaces cheek by jowl in the overwatered lawns above Sunset. Their *marigolds* were worth more than my poor rubies! But I could hold my wealth in my hand or in the tasteful burgundy briefcase under my arm. When I drove up in my ten-year-old Porsche, the ton of metal was in my name and my name alone.

Picture this then: Ms. Langley drives up, stamps up the brick pathway, 11:30 A. M., to a Beverly Hills mansion. Knocks on the door, smiles, waits, is ushered by a servant into the "den." Folds her hands in her lap, talking to the lady of the house. In an extension course, if the class doesn't fill on the first morning, it's goodbye Charlie and come back next semester. But usually a dozen ladies show, between the ages of twenty-seven and sixty. They've taken absolutely every other course: the American and British contemporary novel; interior decorating to avoid allergies, and interior decorating if you *don't* have allergies; conversational French and Spanish, and even the History of Ideas. Let's be straight about it, they all, each and every manicured matron, have a hundred times better education than I. But they have nothing to do, so they show for the class, "because a woman is teaching it," they say.

We sit and chat and, after a few preliminary remarks about American fiscal policy in general, how it is in AT&T's *interest* to make you believe those pieces of paper they called "stock" are valuable—all the while they're looking at me pityingly, because I have to work for a living and they don't—after, as I say, the first twenty minutes, I take a tiny yellow envelope from my decent black purse and shake a half-dozen stones out on the table.

Consternation and more pity. Poor working woman with her pitiable red and green and yellow rocks! (Because, remember, this is Beverly Hills, and these ladies, even on a Wednesday morning, are apt to be decked out like—as my sainted mother used to say—Astor's pet horse.)

But then I screw my loupe in my eye and talk about each stone: the opals the Australian surfer gave me, and how opals exist on art and personal taste alone—in the same category as those pieces of sweet paper AT&T tried to make you believe were money, while *they* kept the money. More glances from the ladies. Don't their husbands have successful investments? And don't they have husbands?

But then I would pick up a great square-cut garnet and talk about polishing, and depth of color, and begin a little rap about what it must have meant to the first caveman when he came upon a stone that glistened, and how, *no matter what happened,* that stone would always glisten. And how that must have been the beginning of "love" as we know it—whatever a woman did to get that first great oaf to give her the stone and *then* to get him to take pride in having given it to her! And the women, one or two of them, might blush or cover a gold bracelet set with diamonds with their deeply tanned hands.

Then, of course, the loupe went around the room, and I always had a couple of extra ones. I saved two loose diamonds for the last—talking that first day about color; how, generally speaking, people said that white, bright white, the excruciatingly lovely absence of color (which was, of course, the *beginning* of color) was "best," but that "cut," of course, mattered too. If you loved the stone, it mattered, and flaws mattered. And the prettier of the two diamonds I passed around had some love attached to it—don't ask me how, it was that way when it came to me—and it had flaws in it. The second diamond that just lay there pokerfaced, the second one anybody might pick up, was flawless. Then I'd show them my earrings. They were *truly something,* and that meant a lot of getting up and going back and forth, because of course I wouldn't take them out, and by that time we'd all be laughing. And I'd tell them that usually the best stones were used for engagement rings and the flawed stones for the ears. Because men had a vested interest.

And someone would ask, or say, helpfully, "You should have some of these other stones *set,* they're so beautiful!" Because by that time they'd be really looking. And I'd say "*No*! I use these to buy and sell and trade. They're not ornaments, they're wealth!"

And I'd stop and smile, to see if they'd *get* it. But they wouldn't, yet. There'd almost always be somebody who'd say, "But wouldn't your husband let . . ."

"Ah," I'd say, "these stones are mine." And then I'd change the subject quickly so as not to hurt their feelings, because they were almost always good women. I'd talk about buying fine stones for their girl children—how they might start with marcasite and coral, *real* things for them to value and keep but not so valuable that the kids would get scared and lose them, and as I'd talk, or during the break, I'd see, out of the corner of my eye, a sweet lady take my loupe and sneak a look at her engagement ring, her bracelet, any of her ordinary daytime jewelry. Other matrons around her would look into the middle distance, and a "girlfriend," because no one ever came to these things alone, would nudge her and ask for a look, and they'd gaze at each other and shrug and exchange disbelieving smiles. "That . . . why that, well, he must not have known." Or sometimes, "That *bastard!*" And even laugh about it.

And we'd spend that first day checking out the jewelry of very wealthy women. Often the flashier it was the more flawed the stones, the more carelessly cut; dirty chips put together in a coruscating mélange that kept you from *knowing* anything about the piece. And always there'd be a woman with one really good stone, and she'd try not to be awful about it. And that would be when I'd reach over into my briefcase and pull out my tenpower microscope that folded up like a spyglass and say, very respectfully, "Do you mind if I take a look at it with this? I'm extremely interested in its density."

I'd fix the stone in the microscope, and give her the first look. Sometimes it was what it appeared to be, but other times that sucker would be as full of holes as a bad Swiss cheese.

"You can't always know," I'd say. "And the people who buy them for you can't always know either."

And there was, of course, the truly gorgeous day when a lady's emerald necklace proved to be pure paste, just as in *Dynasty*, the television show. Watching the divorce proceedings that unfolded on the six o'clock news over a period of months on *that* one, I had the unaccustomed but altogether pleasant sense of having been an active participant in our popular culture.

Mostly, though, the class was for getting those women to pay attention. At the end of twelve weeks, we would have talked of credit and clothes and houses and joint ownership of *things*, and what things made you rich. If I'd made them think, I was happy. If when I left the class at the end, eight out of twelve of those ladies had their own safe deposit boxes and were stacking up, out of "pin" money, those magic little ingots from Macao, if they had bought their daughters second and third strings of fresh water pearls, I had fairly earned the money they paid me.

* * *

MY "LOVE LIFE," AS IT WAS CALLED THEN, WAS ANOTHER story, but I appeared to be as successful in that as in all my endeavors in those years. I did time on yachts, I sat in dress circles, I got and gave pleasure with dutiful enthusiasm.

But there was a refrain in me that said, *Let's get serious*. I had finally learned, somehow, that I was never again going to have to stand around and girlishly accept a single rose or a badly written poem just because somebody had a cute moustache. I couldn't endure to have something explained to me *ever again,* unless it was something I wanted to know.

Now, there were those, and I asked it of myself even then, who might say, what's the big *deal*, lady? Was the lining of your twat made out of Belgian lace, that you could be so picky?

The answer, *no*. But once you start looking for flaws and decide to hoard your wealth rather than squander it, your standards change.

SOMEWHERE IN THE VERY EARLY EIGHTIES, ABOUT A YEAR after I'd come home, I found myself down at a wedding at the yacht club in the marina, looking out of tinted picture windows at boats packed together in a nautical tract, bored with my date and wanting to go home, when I heard someone call my name. Howard "Skip" Chandler had sat in at a meeting a few months before where I'd offered a few common-sense ideas for saving a purse company. Shyly he asked me if I liked my work, and then if I was here alone; if I had children, if I was married. Relentlessly perky, friendly and businesslike, I asked him the same. He was tall, in his sixties, well built, somber, with hazel eyes and black hair just beginning to go grey. His children, he said, lived with their mother in Argentina. He was up here visiting a medical specialist. We went upstairs to the bar, where he tossed back several manhattans, and, gazing at the candle between us as the sun went down behind a zillion sailboats, he talked about wealth, and doom. His wife had insisted on the move south in 1962, during or just after the Cuban crisis. They had dismantled their house—he described this with quiet humor, and somehow I got the impression that he didn't tell this as a "story" very often—and moved, with the children, eight thousand miles south.

After they'd deplaned in Buenos Aires and he'd deposited his frantic wife and tired kids in a suite in the best hotel in town, Skip said he'd gone out for a stroll, to see where it was, exactly, they'd be making their new life.

"I fell in love with the tango," Skip Chandler told me. "Isn't that foolish? I loved the way they sang their songs."

I'd been drinking too, and I knew myself well enough to consider that about now I ought to be excusing myself to call the kids, to say I'd be coming home late.

"As a city, B.A. is very ugly," said Skip. "There's nothing but dirt and car exhaust there, you see. My wife hated it, but she was—I suppose we *all* were, I shouldn't put it just on her—cautious about coming back. You don't move a family eight thousand miles for nothing."

"So, why are you here then?"

I had heard by now, of course, every—what we used to call *line*—devised by man, including one from a huffy and overweight divorce lawyer who had announced very indignantly, "You've gone to bed with everyone else we both know, why not me?"

"You've got to draw the line somewhere," I answered, "and I'm drawing it with you!"

So I listened to Mr. Chandler, trying to keep my loupe in my eye. I heard a story of a life of duty and rectitude, of girls—Charlene and Juanita—grown up and married now to Argentine businessmen; of Deeky, his bachelor son; of a wife ruled by fear, who read the papers each day to see if the human race was still viable for another twenty-four hours, who—during those short wars like the Yom Kippur fracas, had simply gone to bed, because her knees wouldn't hold her up, and turned her face to the wall.

"She's a good woman, the best. She's not a coward, she's brave. She's let herself know, you see, what the rest of us just—don't look at. Every day is a victory for her."

And Skip—what a spunky name for such a somber guy—finding, in some elegant Argentine doctor's office, that he had a dark shadow on his kidney, had elected to come up here for a while. He was involved in international finance, he told me; he was putting together a bank, perhaps for Blacks or Hispanics or—his long lashes lowered as he gazed steadily at the candle in the red glass between us—women, perhaps. Something independent, out of the larger scheme of California finance, with ready money for quick investments.

"Your wife? Does she . . . ?"

"No, she doesn't 'know,' and no, I'm not going to tell her. Because . . . It's not that I'm afraid of what it will do to her. It's . . ."

"Just don't go to UCLA," I blurted. "It's a butcher shop."

Was he telling the truth? Who could tell? We were all great storytellers, even in those days. His suit—a tenebrous grey, was of a conservative cut. His hands were large and angular. I didn't see depression in him, exactly, but he looked as if he'd been hexed. You might see his handsome face and tall frame, feet backwards, strolling along dirt roads at night; a zombie, but a nice one.

"So what's that stuff about the tango?"

"They have nothing down there but music was what I meant to say. They live in apartments on the thirty-fifth story of a building that faces another apartment in another building. But they go out, you see, and down into the streets, to try to find the tango."

"Listen," I said, "would you like to come home and meet my daughters?"

"Let me make arrangements."

He stood up and bowed and moved toward the door of the bar. A tall blonde in her twenties, lovely in a cream-colored blouse, came up to him. Win a few, lose a few, I thought, and tried my best to be cool *and* honest, staring straight at that handsome couple, then turning in my chair to look out at the marina, which—cluttered and unattractive as it was in the day—turned to a field of blindingly beautiful lights by night.

I felt his hand on my waist. "I'll follow you in my car."

We went out into the parking lot. He smiled so sadly at my Porsche, and what it meant, that the feeling I'd had from the moment I'd seen him clicked further into focus; not "love"—far from it, as I think of it now—but a fateful heavy feeling, once again, of coming down in one piece, in one place.

I drove carefully, Van Morrison blaring his "Tupelo Honey" and other repetitive hits, out of the maze of the marina and into Venice, up along the Palisades of Santa Monica, trying to remember what I knew about Buenos Aires.

His morose Mercedes followed my car up the Coast Highway away from lights and we turned into the black canyon. I drove past where the Indians used to fish and drove the last ten miles in a moonless night, until we turned around in a cul-de-sac and looked up at my house.

The kids, as usual, had every light in the place turned on. Usually I would slam into the kitchen with indignation—turning off lights and delivering admonitions as I went—but tonight I made the turn, churned the engine, paused half a second to see that the place looked *charmed*, with golden light pouring from every window like a just-landed space ship. Gunning that heavy grey metal, I drove for all it was worth at about 125 an hour up my steep

driveway and slammed on the brakes. The Mercedes drew
in smoothly beside me. I looked over at him before he
looked over at me.

It was close to eleven at night: The kids watched a black-
and-white movie on Channel 5. Slices of takeout pizza
littered the coffee table; Aurora was on the phone, Denise
snipped scraps of her hair into a Styrofoam cup. The dy-
namic between the two of them was: Denise pushed and
Aurora held firm. That had been going on for ten years—
why should it stop tonight?

"I didn't!"

"You *will.*"

"You can't make me."

"Shut up and *give* me that!"

I went upstairs to change my clothes. Skip sat cautiously
on the couch and leaned into the chalk light of the set.

He could have been one of those nattily dressed men in
the black-and-white film we were watching. I gave him a
beer and pulled up my knees beside him. The girls paid
him the compliment of simply going on with their ageless
game. By one-thirty or two we'd finished off a six-pack,
the kids had gone to bed, and bit by finicky bit we'd finished off the last of the pizza, so that by subtraction the
living room looked almost clean. I looked over at Skip,
ready to tell him that although we hadn't had a "magic
evening," at least it had been a wonderful *night*, and saw
that he'd gone to sleep sitting up. I pushed him sideways.
Still wearing his suit and looking dignified as a cadaver
who'd had his mouth sewn shut, he straightened out on
the couch. I found a quilt to cover him, turned out the
lights, and went upstairs.

Next morning, feeling stiff and nervous, I went down
to tell him he'd have to leave—the girls would never buy
a story about him sleeping on the couch, and they were
morally opposed to anything that looked vaguely like a
one-night stand—only to find him and his Mercedes gone.

I walked out onto the dusty crescent that was our back-yard: that view from here into infinity. But here on the still-new fill where I stood, it was just a matter of getting some petunias I'd planted to grow. I watered them and began to think large thoughts of rosemary and mint in terraces down into the abyss as soon as I could afford the Mexican help, when I heard a smooth motor in the very still morning. I wiped off my hands, turned off the hose, and was there at the top of the driveway when Skip got out of the car.

"You were out of milk and eggs," he said. "And mightn't the girls like some coffee cake?"

He didn't look as good as he had the night before by a long shot. His eyeballs had a bright yellow cast; his face was grey. He was a sick man, no doubt about it. But he came in and had breakfast with us and then excused himself to make some phone calls. He said he'd be out for lunch and the rest of the afternoon. Then in the most courteous possible way, he asked the girls if he might come up again that evening.

"I miss my own family, very much," he told them. "I saw again last night what a delight it is to be in a real home. I wonder if I might return tonight and fix you an Argentine dish, to repay you for last night's hospitality."

So that was *it*! Within a month he'd be living downstairs in what was to have been my office, a ticker tape clicking away in there and an extra bank of phones ringing. And in six months I was a member of the board of what was going to be L.A.'s Third Women's Bank, if Skip's boys could get it off the ground.

Don't ask *me* how it happened—how a man came north (from where his family had gone to escape death) in order to die but instead grounded himself in a living room where the sight of two (ordinary, then, except for how much we loved them) sweet girls at least put into question whether he was going to keel over immediately or put it off for as much as a year.

Under Skip's tutelage, and staked by him at first, I learned how to invest—something I'd always resisted. Now, I had money out there working for me.

But money was only the metaphor. Looking at my stones, sometimes in the afternoons, with the sun pouring in and the leaves outside gently blowing about and Skip closeted with his clicking tape, I'd touch those smooth, cool, bright, hard, valuable surfaces and think—*if I could be like you!* Because nothing can harm you! And looking at my low and sullen silver Porsche with the engine that could kill by noise alone, *if I could be like you!*

Stasis was what I craved and what I got, thinking it was safety. If anyone had mentioned politely that I might be dead at the center I would have answered, "So?" That was what I was aiming at. I was a stone; I was a rock; I had come down hard.

2

JUNE 1981

LIVING WITH SKIP, WORKING ON THE HOUSE, "WATCHING
our money grow," as they said on the television commercials—all of that was powerfully comforting. Sometimes
I'd look across the living room; I'd be on the loveseat and
Skip would be on the couch, and the two girls would be
on either side of him, not fighting for once but snuggling
into his dignified form, and a fairly standard set of anxiety
attacks would play over me: He's not their father! I should
find some *real* guy to get married to! What about sex?
Because of this impetuous attachment to a dying man, was
I doomed to live the life of a celibate for the next thirty-
five years of my life? Shouldn't I be *out* somewhere, grab-
bing some glamour?

But it was so extremely pleasant, so sensible and strange
to live in a house with a man (of whatever variety), and
children, that I couldn't bring myself to change it. (That's
another story, isn't it? A single woman with children goes
out fishing in the vast seas of the city. She gets a tug on
her line and brings someone home, gasping. She flings
her catch on the kitchen sink. Is it a shark, or a prince?
This may not be a popular story, or even a very interesting
one, but a lot of the women I knew lived it.)

I knew Skip had his own family. Charlene, Juanita,

27

Deeky. "Very conservative," Skip would say about his son. "A good Catholic." About his wife he said little. A couple of times she called the house but on the downstairs phone, which by now was a branch of Chandler Enterprises. I answered it that way, but if I knew who *she* was, dollars to doughnuts she knew about me. On the other hand, so what? Skip and I didn't even share the same bed, his eyes were as yellow as daffodils, and we were all ten years older than God anyway. So it went on.

One night, after the girls had gone to bed, he did accounts while I read a book and crunched on Triscuits. When he looked up, I stopped chewing.

"I'm sorry. Am I driving you crazy?"

"No, dearheart," he said. "I was just wondering— please say no if you don't like the sound of it—would you *really* like to be a bank president? Because the money is there, now."

The Third Women's Bank of Santa Monica. I would be the president, and there would be women on *both* sides of the bank as the customer went in, but I would still be the only woman on the board, as an attractive token. Most of the money would be coming from out of the country, out of the hemisphere.

He cloaked his offer in apologies. But my mind was full of thoughts of sudden power, the dreams of a single mother with children. Harvard, not a junior college, for my two daughters. Trust funds for all; not just a condominium, but a *villa* in Hawaii for my declining years.

I learned to say nothing in meetings, letting my earrings speak for me; I was nothing but a pair of jeweled ears, allowing the words of smart, rich men to sink in. It was a nasty jolt, smiling through four hours at a time in the company of men whose only concern was getting and spending. Yet, as these geezers—young and old—cheerfully sent small businesses to their doom and ground their teeth over, say, "affordable housing," I took some com-

fort from their behavior. Their awfulness was magnifi-
cently impersonal. They meant nothing by it, and who was
I to challenge the iron rules of masculine commerce?

I learned a lot. And Skip, for the hell of it, leased a
Lear jet. We zipped up as far north as Vancouver, as far
south as Panama (no farther), but never east. It was Skip's
idea—certainly not new, even then—that Europe was dead,
that the new markets were on the Pacific rim. He loved
the idea of cheap Asian labor. When you talked to Skip
you got the idea that in Hong Kong, Taipei, even, they
worked seventeen-hour days, then stayed up all night and
danced. Because under his sedate blazer and his knobby
chest, there beat a heart, remember, that loved the tango.

With all this I kept on teaching my extension courses,
and grew ever more stern. Everything I learned I passed
on to those ladies. I had my picture taken to go at the top
of the finance column I wrote for the "second" newspa-
per. (The first still wouldn't take it—a secret humiliation
to me.)

One Friday morning in early summer we got into the
Porsche and careened down to the Santa Monica airport.
It was a clean, sunny day, the kids were visiting their dads
for a long weekend. We were flying to San Francisco for
the same amount of time. There would be a couple of
afternoon meetings with some of those heavy, anonymous
men Skip loved to court and then a weekend seminar—it
might be a pyramid scheme—that the paper had suggested
I go up and "expose." A young northern California confidence man named Lion Boyce had gotten himself written
up in *Money* magazine; he was rumored to espouse all
kinds of crooked behavior and to recruit mush-minded
young people by the strength of his charisma. The state of
California was investigating his enterprises, and it was inevitable that he should fail. Since the second paper was
failing every day, in comparison to the *L.A. Times*, it took
great pleasure in pointing out how the rest of the world

was failing too. I looked forward to this assignment for my own reasons; since so much of my own "career" was based on con, I hoped to pick up a few pointers.

Our pilot that day suffered from a bad disposition and a crashing hangover. When he hit the Frisco fog, zooming—it seemed—straight down, I quavered, through the open door, "What's the visibility?" He answered, gravel-voiced, shimmying the damn thing, I swear, just to make me more terrified, "How do I know?" The plane sliced through fog like a hot knife through clotted cream. I put the faces of my two children in my mind, looked over at Skip, and saw him smiling. The stupid fool! He *wanted* to die!

Then we saw the world again—the bay itself skimming the landing gear. We whiffled just above that shifting blue surface, climbed out of clear air into fog again, so that we could hit the runway. "I know, I *know,*" our hungover and spiteful pilot grumbled into his radio, "yes, I'll file one."

When our feet touched ground, even Skip looked sheepishly relieved. We had lunch in a tourist attraction—a Hungarian restaurant high up in a tower above the bay. By then the fog had lifted. We ate fried bread with scraped raw garlic and drank white wine.

I want to make the point here that, even though the world had not yet started to be magic, it was still swell enough *just the way it was* that even Skip and I noticed it that day. We'd come close to dying; maybe that was why the very air up here smelled so sweet. I'd been raised a Catholic and didn't, of course, believe anymore, but I remember thinking, If there's no Heaven at all, this is still pretty good.

After our meetings, we went up to our room at the Clift to change and saw the flowers and the fruit they had waiting for us. The light of the dying sun caught at two double gin martinis that Skip had ordered up.

He said, "When I think that Estelle let herself lose all this, just because of fear, I . . . feel so sorry."

What could I say? I was just damn glad that woman was eight thousand miles away and likely to stay there, because even as we'd gone through the lobby, there'd been the usual raft of newspapers with horrible headlines, and even though I knew now those scavengers used their black words just to sell their dubious product, still, somebody out there was doing *something*. It was just possible that, nutty as she was, Estelle was going to be right.

WITH WHAT FEELINGS OF SUPERIORITY THE AILING FINAN-cier and I climbed the stairs that night in a second-rank San Francisco hotel, surrounded by leftover hippies and gibbering faggots and heterosexuals who couldn't keep their hands off each other, some of whom *already* smelled bad, even though the weekend hadn't even started. The yellow-carpeted mezzanine was mayhem, filled with al-umni of this weekend, and guests, and seminar-shoppers, and all manner of "assistants," some of whom demon-strated their unfamiliarity with the English alphabet as they tried to look up paid reservations, and some, on roller skates, who left tracks behind them in the nylon nap as they swooped past. Some carried megaphones and pom-poms.

We stood nervously at one of several card tables covered with nicely lettered name cards. Girls with names like Rain, Rainbow, Sunset, and Sparrow, all of them beaming like fools, took our coats, pinned on our names, handed us brochures, and shooed us into a medium-sized confer-ence room, already full of the penniless and unemployed, having spent, some of them, their rent money, their last dollar, in an attempt to get rich quick without working, and have some fun along the way.

Lion Boyce's seminar brochure was flimsy and full of

misspellings. It promised that we would lose weight, quit smoking, find the perfect mate, and triple our income in a year, if we followed the principles laid out during this weekend. The last page was loaded with hazards and disclaimers. No money would be refunded to those who left early or—later in the year—those who could not prove they'd been using the principles. Also: "**Participants will be required not to reveal the contents of this weekend and will be also required to sign a pledge to stay in attendance until the seminar ends." (Two promises I fully intended to break as soon as possible.) And "**Participants are requested, for their own comfort and convenience, to wear loose clothes."

As the room was still filling up and people hesitated over which was the best folding chair to sit in, an amiable, puffyfaced young man in a purple velvet suit with a yellow rose in his lapel pranced up through the middle aisle and began a cheery tirade, mincing and grimacing and flicking his hands at us: "You saw one world as you came in here. *Believe* me, you'll see another one when you go out. You sportsmen! Who ever said you couldn't run a one-minute mile! Lion will show you how!" And I remember wondering how I could make a column out of that.

When Lion Boyce came out, I saw he was young enough to be my son. He wore a dazzling white linen suit, and his pale skin flushed girlishly along the cheekbones. He walked lightly on the balls of his feet and there was something absent in him. He was sure no financial wizard: after days of watching the big boys play, I knew that. I glanced over at Skip and saw him smiling at this audacious boy. In fact, we were, already, in another world. There was plenty of time later to worry about criminal intent.

They opened with a simple parlor game about money as "energy" and how some people just naturally win. Skip and I naturally won and felt pretty smug about it. Then Lion Boyce watched as his toothsome assistants skated in and unfurled a small movie screen for an eight-millimeter film. "I saw this a few months ago," he said, and you sensed how close his voice still was to the memory of breaking. "I liked it a lot. It shows how the universe works."

The lights went out and a dreadful sound track began. In smudged black-and-white we were shown a black spot in a white field. "This freckle," the sound track boomed, "this *freckle* is on the shoulder of a man lying face down at the beach. If we move away, to the power of ten," and, as the track said it, the camera moved to show an unattractive man, a wrinkled blanket, a picnic basket, "we see that . . ." The camera flashed and flashed again, to the power of ten, showing us the city of Tampa, the state of Florida, the earth, the galaxy, and then the film was through and the lights went up. The audience—failures, most of them, at *everything*—looked haunted. None of them had ever been able to answer questions about classroom films; that was one reason why they'd blundered, this weekend, into this last strange spasm of San Francisco consciousness-raising.

But Lion Boyce's points were simple, and he spelled them out. This was an expanding universe—scientifically proven fact!—and if you decided you wanted something, and remembered the idea of expansion, you might get it. You might turn your dented Volks into a Cadillac, or parlay your tugboat into a fleet. Lion also took the film to mean that this was "one universe" and he a cosmic, "one-world," Wendell Willkie.

"What you do *here*," Lion said, wiggling his left arm, "is apt to show up over here," and wiggled his right. "You could think of it as Jell-O. Like, the cosmos is red Jell-O." The audience blinked.

I thought something like that might be a good reason why people on the East Coast thought we were nuts. But up in front, another man, with a guitar, had already come out. He began a little talk about—what else?—*conscious-ness*. He talked about "singing the blues," and I thought what an intelligent way that was to address an unlettered crowd about their thought processes, because everyone listened to their radios, everyone had hummed along since they were tots, "I can't get no satisfaction!" And suddenly I thought of my second ex-husband: *No pain, no gain! Nothing good is easy!* He really believed that stuff—he said it all the time!

Then the man with the guitar began to sing, off-key:

Abundance is My Natural State!
I Love to Participate!
Abundance is My Natural State!

They expected us to sing. My cheeks burned with embarrassment.

But damned if some little Japanese girl didn't get up then and say she couldn't sing and *wouldn't* sing, because our world was a cruel one. Her mother had been a Hiroshima maiden. She cried when she said it. The man in the white suit smiled calmly. "That's radiation. But there's another kind," he said. "What about *I am a blazing sun of infinitely abundant energy flooding forth the limitless treasures of light for the good of one and all?*"

A few people walked out. A couple of people asked (cogently, I thought) how this was going to help them make good financial investments. But Lion Boyce said that we were going to have to stand up and move out into the aisle. The guitar started again. And all those hippie-girl "assistants" came in to dance, showing us by gestures that they wanted us to dance too.

I remembered that snotty East Coast photographer of jumps. So I only had *one*, the filthy little prick! I began a quiet, solo two-step.

"If you don't dance," Lion Boyce said to the assembled

crowd with sweet reasonableness, "how do you expect to have any *fun*?"

When we got out of breath and sat down again, Lion went on to talk about energy—electricity. He showed us slides of Kurlean photography (which I still believe were fake) but he convinced me completely about negative energy. "Didn't you ever know a Wet-Blanket-Louie? You're feeling fine, and someone comes in the door, and all of a sudden it's like the light went out?" He had my second husband down to a tee.

Once again it was time to get up. "It's no big deal," Lion Boyce said, "but just—hold out your arm. And extend the energy. Don't work at it!" (Because some women were frowning and some men huffing with the strain of putting their arms out there and making them strong.) "Just put out about twelve inches or so of shining light, out from the end of your fingers. Now divide into groups of two. Now the A person, hold out that arm! Wrap it in radiant energy to make it invincible."

I looked up at Skip and his sorrowful extended arm.

"Now, B persons, swing on that arm. *Don't work at it!* Let the energy take care of it."

Could I really lean on Skip? Could I put my weight, *all my weight,* on someone else, a *man?* What the hell, it was only a game. This was just a hotel room. I reached up and swung. Across the room I saw the daughter of the Hiroshima maiden, swinging. She looked cautious.

"Now, B people, extend your arm and visualize the energy *no, don't work at it*! Just think it. A people . . ."

I weighed 130 at the time; Skip was 185. But he swung from my arm.

"Only in San Francisco!" somebody said, and walked out. And another person called Lion Boyce a fag, and left. And another several people said it was rigged and accused us—Skip and me!—of being shills. But by then the rest of us had forgotten everything except the wonder of swinging on each other's arms.

Lion looked detached. "It's interesting," he said, "that if you hold some refined sugar on your hand, you can't do it as easily. But if you hold a ten-dollar bill, or a hundred . . ." And soon, at the front of the room, a group of younger men had crowded around Lion, balancing chairs and tables on their (relaxed) arms.

All this on the first night, a plain Friday night.

The thirty or so of us left around midnight were still trying to "get" it, so to say, although I deplore the use of that word in that way.

"You *really* mean that—what you think—has something to do with what happens to you?"

And I remembered all the times I'd looked at my second husband and thought: You vicious little creep. And he was!

"Not just what you think," the boy, Lion, was explaining. "What you *say,* as well. How about, 'I'm dying for a drink'? 'I'm going to flunk that test'? Or, 'You don't love me! You never have and you never will!' "

A couple of us began to get a little weepy.

"A day late and a dollar short," somebody muttered behind me. "They said I was just like my father," a young guy said. "And you know what? I *was.*"

"Now, if you were to apply some of this to finance," Lion said briskly, "which we'll get into tomorrow, you can see where that kind of thinking might get in your way a little."

By one in the morning, still in that hotel room, dizzy with fatigue and high as a kite, I sat opposite my friend. We'd just told each other if we could "be, do, or have anything that we wanted," what it would be. Skip had alternately told me that he'd wanted to die, to live to be a hundred, to leave his family forever, to have his family with him forever. Then we turned and changed partners; it was getting to be too much. But we turned to each other

again as Lion wrote on the blackboard: *I am a powerful,
loving and creative person, and I can handle it, and I can
have anything I want.*

The lights went down, the assistants put on some corny
music. "I am a powerful, loving, creative . . ."

We took turns saying it, while the other one said, "Yes,
I know." Skip's face floated and faded in the darkness. I
saw his glittering teeth. A frantic warning went up inside
me—this is fake, this is silly, this is hypnotism, what about
war, what about *Dan Rather!*

I thought of Dan Rather, fixing millions of apprehensive
Americans with his meaningful gaze, opening his mouth
and saying, "I am a powerful, loving, and creative person, and I can handle it, and I can have anything I want."
Some people around me were crying. The voices of this
litany went on for what must have been a half hour, and
they were inexpressibly sweet.

Then it was over, the lights went up. "Let me remind
you," the boy in white said. "You've only had one night
of this. And a whole life lived the other way. So . . . check
it out. Just check it out."

We took a cab back to the Clift. The old hotel was so
exquisite, the waiters and bellboys so silly in their uniforms, their faces so human and new. We went upstairs in
the elevator. I was thinking about Sylvia Plath, and Skip
said later he was nearly frantic about supply and demand.
What might this crack-brained way of thinking do to *Ro-
meo and Juliet?* To John Maynard Keynes?

The maids had been in to turn down our bed, the lamp
was lit, and champagne waited for us. Ordinarily on these
hotel nights, Skip would put on his pajamas, I'd skin into
one of his shirts. We'd pull up in bed like kids on a slumber party, watching old movies, drinking until we slept.

But tonight he turned off the light and brought over the
champagne in the dark. I thought, with a clutch at my
stomach, that I'd turned away from Skip to tell a stranger

that if I could have anything I wanted it would be a lover who would love me back. (As if I ever in my life could have handled such a thing!) *No,* I thought frantically, *really,* I changed my mind. I'd rather not!

His face was closed and frightened and far away. He looked like the daughter of the Hiroshima maiden, hanging from an obliging human arm, her small feet swinging an inch or two above the carpet, and suddenly I thought, What the Hell! This was just a hotel room! I thought of one of the early "affirmations" Lion had suggested at the beginning of the evening: "Every dollar I spend comes back to me vastly multiplied! And that's OK!" I reached out, grabbed Skip, pulled him down to me.

Late that night, Skip heaved himself up on an elbow and looked at me seriously. "Are you sure we've done the right thing? I never wanted to hurt you. Remember, I'm a dying . . ." As I started to laugh, he looked disgusted and undignified and irritated. "Well, *shit,*" he said. And I'd never heard him use that word before, "Well, God *damn* it!"

WE WENT BACK THE NEXT MORNING, WREATHED IN smiles. Lion Boyce told us about the "hokeyness barrier," that awful thing that kept us from *playing* when we wanted to, that kept us impersonating grown-ups when we didn't need to—the thing that kept our children in constant embarrassment for *us.* He held a green hand puppet to impersonate the voice inside us that says, "You mean you're going outside the house wearing *that?*" Or, I remembered, my ex-husband's father saying, after my husband had taken apart a watch, "Oh, he can take them apart, but he can't put them together again." Or my mother: "Must you be so clumsy?" How we took that voice and locked it inside ourselves. I flashed on the streets of New York, every person striding about: Don't mug me! I am a serious

person! Watch my briefcase! Watch my boots! Watch my
. . . ! Yes, but out *here,* how many people bellied up to
how many languid bars in how much white linen; their
silent message—"I'm cool! I'm cool! Don't mess with me,
I'm cool!"

It was this boy's contention, then, that we could "be,
do, and have" exactly what we wanted. That we were a
part of a vast energy field, that we could turn this energy
any way we wanted to. That Christ had only been doing
what any one of us could do. But that we had to have the
guts to try it; that's why Christ walked on the water and
that other guy sank.

But Lion took the position—as did so many other California evangelists—that "the universe always said yes."

So that if you said, "l'm afraid," you were. Or, "I look
so awful . . ." You get the picture. But if you said, "The
whole universe is supporting and assisting me! I am successful at everything I do," and *if you kept* saying it . . .

"Cosmic Jell-O," he kept saying. "Just think of the
universe as red Jell-O."

We spent the rest of the morning either thinking ourselves "heavy," so that it took seven of us to lift one little
teenager off the ground, or "light," so at one point two
of us ladies lifted some big bruiser up off the ground with
one hand each. We were given to understand that if we
didn't use our own energy, but kept on using the real stuff,
the *big* stuff, we could do almost anything.

Early Christian beliefs, common sense, American pos-
itive thinking and some half-baked Eastern semithought.
It was all derivative: While I was making myself heavy, I
knew that *babies* knew how to do this from their third
month, when they didn't want to be picked up, they developed an affinity for the ground. But what Lion had,
what my friend Lorna Villanelle would pick up later, and
what his followers loved him for, was—just the fun.

"Does anyone want to 'share' what might have happened since last night?'' the warm-up man in the purple suit suggested during a break, and all over the room people raised their hands and said things like their car wouldn't start but then they talked to it and then it did. Or a cop had stopped them, but they'd given him a big smile and he'd gone away without giving them a ticket. A mother stood up and said, ''I've been having a hard time supporting my children. I've been on welfare. I had to scrape together the money to get here. I thought, part of the time that you—that Lion—was swindling us last night. But,'' and here, her face, though its expression didn't change, glistened with tears, ''I went home and just went in and looked at my kids, and I saw such wealth . . .''

Lion, on the sidelines, looked mildly pleased. ''As long as you think you're going to get swindled, that's going to happen,'' and he went into a diatribe about those poor fools in this world who watched Cal Worthington on television, and drove down to some ten-acre used-car place, and waddled in with the sense of a duck, no more than that—''Quack, quack,'' he said, and he *was* a duck, ''Do you have a car for us, mister?''

I memorized his principles, though he didn't ask us to. Each new thing he wanted us to learn he'd had typed out on a handful of papers (full of more misspellings), which his assistants (some of them chunky and funny looking but all of them transfixed with happiness) held high over their heads and roller-skated out to us, waving pompoms and cheering.

''Listen,'' Lion said, ''if you ever expect to get anything, you've got to give it away first. Everything you give away comes back to you vastly multiplied! That's called *outflowing!*'' (And after I'd sent my kids to the ''training'' one of their favorite pastimes was leaving quarters in pay-phone slots.)

But listen! If you're going to get on with a better life, you've got to get rid of the old one! We spent the middle of the day writing down all the awful things we'd ever done, or had done to us. And all the awful things that could happen. The death of my children, World War III, and breast cancer came up one, two, and three on my list. But after an hour of that Lion said, with all the solemnity it deserved, "Now I want you to look those lists over and check that you haven't left anything out. And now I want you to . . . take those sheets and . . . wad them up! Yes, scrunch them up! Now throw them up in the air! See how *light* they are; why you could say, 'My past is now complete! I bless and release it! Wow! I am free and clear!' And listen. This is very important. You don't have to write that stuff down, you know. All you have to do is jack it up into the air, and wrap it in pink light and float it away. It's easy. Now, throw that junk away. Just give it a toss!" (And that was *Clearing.*)

"Of course you have to be trustworthy," Lion said. "If you don't do what you say you're going to do, well, how can you believe anybody else?" That's *Integrity.* Sneakily I remembered I'd done some things I shouldn't. Oh well.

What about some *Goals?* Assuming you really could be, do, and have exactly what you wanted, what would it be? We changed partners and asked each other that one, over and over. It surprised me that, sure, I wanted to be bank president and have a portfolio and security for my children—and look, I already had a wonderful lover!—but "it kept coming up," as they used to say, that I wanted to go to the beach, spend time at the beach, just lie down and look at the ocean. My partner wanted to go to Oregon and raise pigs.

Almost every man in that little room, broke as they were, had put a new car on his list of goals. So Lion told us about treasure maps! "Go down to the car store, find the one you want. Say, 'That's my car!' Cut out a picture of the car. Put a snapshot of yourself in it." *Imaging.*

Skip unexpectedly stood up. "I've always wanted to go

to Alaska, but somehow I've never found the time." Lion gave him a cool appraising stare and, reading from his name tag, said, "Howard Chandler is radiantly aglow with perfect health. When he goes to Alaska he has a wonderful time and doesn't even catch a cold. What do you think?" *Affirming.*

What a con artist Lion was, even then. How like my father, who had once pointed out to me, "If you keep them laughing, you can get into their pants every time." In illustrating the principle of *Wu Wei*, the serenity of the martial arts masters, how you didn't have to "kick and bite and scratch" to attain your goals, Lion introduced us to the Canton Brothers, who in their haste to rape the lovely "Kung Fu Mama," knocked each *other* out. You don't have to try, Lion said. You don't have to worry about it. Things go on happening whether you worry or not.

Decreeing! We all stood up, said what we wanted, raised our hands skyward from that second floor, and decreed it! "I want us to be together forever," Skip said, "God forgive me. So be it, for so it is!"

You can see that at that point Lion Boyce could have suggested that success and happiness come from scrubbing the floor with a toothbrush and we would have run out to Thrifty Drug to corner the market. But he'd started with fifty-two in the seminar the night before, twenty-five had shown up that morning, and he went down to seventeen in five minutes when his assistants skated out with the next mimeographed sheets for *Enthusiasm!* Not fake enthusiasm. The real thing. We all nodded our heads until he turned a couple of effortless cartwheels, landed on his feet—my, he was physically beautiful—and called out, "OOOOeeee! *I see abundance everywhere!*" And could we do something like that, one at a time? No. After some heated arguments, and tipped-over chairs, the room began to empty. My mother's tom-tom voice began: Heav-y! Heav-y! But we did it.

What about war, poverty, disease, the third world?
Lion shrugged.

Persistence. Well, I knew about that.

Concentration. Any working mother knows.

Meditation. Every person in the room closed his or her eyes. No problem.

By the end of that evening every bone in my body ached, I felt I had lived a hundred years. Skip aged and *un*aged.

At about quarter to one that morning, Lion led us in another meditation. "Just let go, relax, let your stomach hang out, who cares? You're fine the way you are. Your deeds, your good works, are beyond compare, and the world loves you for it. I can hear them now, don't you? Aren't they applauding? Yes! They're down there in the street, they want to give you a party! You deserve it!" And the sound swelled of crowds cheering. He told us to open our eyes and we did, to a bevy of sappy assistants with gales of confetti and blowing horns: Happy New Year.

Skip and I kissed in the cab, snaking back through a new world, magic San Francisco. We had the man drive through the Haight, that little street that had gone through acid-magic and heroin-death and now glimmered late at night halfway between the two. More lovemaking, more champagne, more sweet kisses, more laughing out loud until the management called at three in the morning to say there had been complaints. But what if life *was* a party? What if that was not a *theoretical* position? What if, no, really, listen to me—well, I know *you* listen to me. I'm talking to the others who went inland when the time came because they were so sure the world was serious.

Skip talked about it that night, in bed. "What," he said, "if this were really true, not for us, but really?" Later, when we got home, we wondered about that reality. Because, Skip said, look at Hitler, or Mussolini, or even the Kennedys. There wasn't a cartwheel in any of them. But the other side of it was that you never saw Lion Boyce

laughing either. There was a cold, cutting edge to everything he said. "You turkeys!" must have been Christ's
unspoken statement as he walked across the water, and
the people he was rescuing were even his friends. Also, a
lot was riding on the other vision. (Later, when Lorna
Villanelle had her picture up in New York subways with
the caption, *God loves you and so do I,* I know more than
one irate rider must have muttered, "Who is that cunt?"
But our current president could predict millions of deaths
in the defense of democracy and those same grown-ups
nodded sagely and reelected him.)

When we went back to the seminar on Sunday morning
there were only eight people left. All we had to learn that
third day was *Realizing:* "It" was already there, with us,
in us, everything we wanted; we *were* what we wanted,
the earth was our toy.

"I am a blazing sun of infinitely abundant energy flooding forth the limitless treasures of light for the good of
one and all!" *Sourcing* was Lion's final point. "Suppose
your body was a tank," Lion said. "You're up there inside, *you're* driving the tank!"

By this time most of the assistants had come into the
room from the outer closet where they had been changing
costumes. They still had on their roller skates and clutched
big handfuls of balloons. So wacked out when first we'd
seen them, they seemed now perfectly OK, *normal.* Most
of them were women, attracted, of course, to Lion, and
they clustered and skittered along the sides of the room,
playing with energy fields, ratcheting around on roller
skates.

And it was time, again, to do that exercise: "If you
could be, do, or have, anything you wanted, what would
it be?" Skip and I faced each other again:

To love Somebody, and be loved.

Yes, I know.

Oh, how we smiled at each other!

To have my children live to be a hundred! To have beautiful grandchildren!

Yes, I know.

To be rich. To have everything I want.

Yes, I . . .

To spend more time at the beach?

Yes, I . . .

But then I felt an explicable stab, and those ever-easier tears. "You know what, Skip? I . . . don't laugh, I work pretty hard, and I . . . I've lost my friends, you know? just someone to call on the phone, in the middle of the morning? Like . . . a girlfriend? I . . . A *friend?*"

Yes, I know.

And he said he wanted to be well forever, to live to be a hundred, to know his family was safe, to travel to Alaska, spend more time at the beach, and die in my arms, but not for a long time.

Yes, I said, *I know.*

Then the assistants came skating past one last time with big yellow binders for us to wrap our list of "principles" in. By that time—since the sixties were in living memory and this was San Francisco—some of them had been playing in the makeup pretty heavily. A woman with flaming red hair flecked with sequins, eyelids heavily encrusted with glitter, leaned in with a binder and grabbed my shoulder.

"Edith? *Edith?* Is it *you?* It's Lorna! Lorna McAvey. Lorna Sullivan. Lorna La Boeuf. Lorna Israel. Don't you remember me? L.A. State College? How are you? I *thought* it was you! I just flew in this morning. Sunday's the best day, don't you think? This is *fun,* isn't it? It's better than that semantics class we were in! Say, do you ever see Marina Bokelman? Do you ever see that one-note composer, what's-his-name? How are the kids?"

It was time for the very last "process." We pulled up chairs in fours, and the assistants came in to join us. Three of us took turns looking at the fourth and saying in unison, "I behold you with eyes of love, You Radiant Being, You!" And the fourth, the "radiant being," got to say, *"Mmm, thank you."* Skip and I, Lorna and a pregnant girl, made up our foursome. At the end of a half hour or so of taking turns, they had to call an ambulance for the girl, her unborn kid got so excited. Lorna pulled her knees up under her.

"So, how are the *kids?* What are you doing now? Do you live up here? I flew in from L.A. . . . isn't that *crazy?* I try not to miss these things. Isn't that guy a kick? I love him, I do. I'm working over at UCLA as a research assistant, what are you doing?" Then, whispering in my ear, "Who *is* that guy? He is *cute!* Does your husband know? You divorced *Dirk?* Well, good riddance! I *hated* that guy!" And at three or so in the morning, standing outside the hotel, we exchanged addresses and phone numbers. Her last words were, "Call me!"

And I did.

Now, you could say I didn't want to "be, do or have" enough. I didn't ask for a chain of hotels, or a small African country to rule over, or, even, to weigh in at ninety-nine pounds forever. Or, what about world peace? I guess I just forgot.

BACK IN L.A., SKIP FINALLY MADE AN APPOINTMENT TO go in to the doctor. "If I'm going to live to be a hundred, I suppose I might as well get down to it." But he found, of course, that there was absolutely nothing wrong with him. The doctor was quite impatient, and said no, there was *nothing,* there was no question of a cure because there was no shadow, no nothing anywhere at all; there must have been a faulty machine in the other doctor's office, down in Buenos Aires.

And I lost my column in Los Angeles' second news-

paper. I went sailing in with a thousand words of good
advice about Xeroxing hundred-dollar bills just for the fun
of it and pasting them up around the room, and throwing
kisses at the cars you wanted on the freeway, and of course
they turned it down flat. "Have you gone *crazy?*" my
editor said. He was a beige little man, my size.

"No, wait. Just watch. Now hold your arm out. Now,
clench your fist! Now, *work* on it! Now, *watch.*" And with
my little finger, beaming like sixty, I pushed down his
clenched fist, his muscled arm. Then, I made him hang
on my arm. Then he said, "He sure fooled *you,* honey!"
And I said, "Oh, yeah? Well listen to this! I happen to
know that that guy is out there *right now* skydiving through
the air with six beautiful women, and one of them is one
of my very oldest and best friends, and where are you,
huh? I don't see *you* out skydiving! I don't see *you* so
fucking rich! I see you in an office without any *windows,*
that's where *you* are!"

So I didn't have the column any more.

In the weeks that followed, Skip and I took a cruise to
Alaska. He didn't even catch cold. I doubled my money.

I pushed the kids into the "Training"; they began getting A's in school and laughing a lot. We had this in common: We'd see a "Wet-Blanket-Louie" and nudge each
other. Or I'd do a martyr act, or Skip would do a dead
act, but the acts wouldn't last long because we were all
onto each other.

We started, all four of us, trying to figure out what it
was we really wanted. That wasn't as easy as it sounds.

We learned to keep quiet about all this material. People
didn't want to hear it.

And then, of course, it receded into the past—the universe to the power of ten, the lost freckles on the man who
was lying out there at the beach.

Every morning Lorna and I managed to talk for a while
on the phone.

"You know what, kid?" And she'd still say *kid* with that touching confidence, that air of confidentiality, that we'd had together when we were young wives, "I think I've paid my debt to society. I'm in it for the fun now, and that's all I'm in it for."

You know what we didn't talk about until much, much later? Lion, or what she did in all those trainings. And I never mentioned what I knew about her from college. Even after all we thought we knew, there was some embarrassment. I still feel that embarrassment, telling it to you now.

3 ~

FEBRUARY-JUNE 1962

ONE JUMP, ONE STORY; TWO WOMEN TO ONE STORY.
There used to be a phrase we had in junior high school—
girls might be "joined at the hip." You never heard that
about boys! And you never saw boys get up and go to the
powder room in pairs either.

When we first went to college, when we traveled, when
we married, there was the feeling that all that might
change, should change.

But some things never change, and I know women who
have survived divorce handily but mourned for years over
the death of a friend, or a friendship.

When we were kids, we'd walk in twos, threes, or fours,
singing, "We ain't got a barrel of *money!* Maybe we're
ragged and *funny!* But we'll travel *along,* singing a *song,*
side by side!" Never even considering that the larger world
didn't give a rat's ass whether we traveled side by side or
not.

And many times my first husband's face isn't clear to
me, but I'll remember, for instance, little Nancy Stone
playing what she was pleased to call gnip gnop on the
cement Ping-Pong tables under wide shady trees at Thomas
Starr King Junior High School until I die.

Why do I waste time reiterating this? Because most

women forget to say it, or didn't notice it when it was happening, or if we felt that way, discounted it. It couldn't be correct, that way of thinking, because men, or if not men, children, or if not children, houses, were important. Nancy Stone, aged fourteen, playing gnip gnop was absolutely—on the face of it—*not important*.

Very near to the end of the world, or the beginning, I went to a baby shower attended by career ladies who had waited until their thirties to go ahead and do what we'd jumped into halfway through our college years. I'm talking inexpensive but beautiful pottery and painted metal bookcases; an interior *sans* reproach, and even though every woman there made "good money" instead of keeping house, the equation was exactly the same: a seriousness, a looking sideways at each other—Are we in step? Are we singing the right tune? Are we doing it right? And outside, visible from time to time, two pairs of muscular bare shoulders of *the men*, laying a brick patio. And only after we'd eaten all our melon balls, and the mother-to-be had opened the gifts, and we'd drunk up the champagne did the hostess begin to *loll* a little bit, and we all told in-law stories, and hunchback jokes, and talked about sex, and the serious married part of it went out the window and for a few hours every lady said silently, The hell with it! Let's play gnip gnop.

When I was first married, in the late fifties, my husband and I were poor. My baby daughter wore pink corduroy overalls and crawled furiously until she wore holes through pink corduroy knees. I made casseroles. But I had ambition, for what, I didn't know. It was a disease that had begun to afflict young women; a plague. If only we could have been content to compete in terms of desserts and casseroles and whose kid spoke in complete sentences first!

Of course we did all that but it wasn't enough.

I met Lorna at Los Angeles State College in the first years of its existence. Twelve quonset huts on a vacant lot in an East L.A. barrio, and that was the best it *ever* looked. Good sweet men (with Brand X Ph.D.'s and inexpensive suits), who had fought in the Korean war, sat in those quonset huts while new, thin, green threads of grass tried to hold their beachhead outside. Those men told us about Hemingway as if they'd only just heard of him, and a sociologist told us that a lot of female typists typing for a male boss didn't mean men and women were working *well* together, and a "bonehead" biologist told us that if you gave an accident victim a transfusion of the wrong blood type he was just as dead as if he had died in a nuclear war. They were always telling you something like that. The truth is, I see now, they had no more clue—in those jerry-built shelters as tentative as this morning's new mushrooms—of education than we had of adulthood. They had an *idea* of how things should go but few facts at their disposal.

I've often thought since then that intellectuals pick their slant in life in the same way that psychiatrists used to pick their profession because they were crazy. We were *out of it*—all of us that I knew anyway—taking mindless advantages of loopholes in the system, the G.I. Bill, the slight dip in the postwar population, an absentmindedness on the part of the ruling classes. Like bamboo, we'd found holes in the system and were growing up through them, though if you asked a piece of bamboo three or four inches high what its plans were in life, you know the kind of answer you'd get.

I like to think I was "unconscious" then, which is why I, who had "quit school to get married" and even traveled for a year in Europe, found myself now with an artist husband and a load of "ambition" which must have been very much like a hard-on. I couldn't get rid of it, it made me look ridiculous, it had to *go* somewhere, and so I decided to "go back to school." On Tuesdays and Thursdays I went to that state college, taking fifteen units in two days, choosing at that time a major in the humanities—so far away in mind and body and imagination were women from the world of power and money. I see now, of course, I was flexing my knees to jump.

I don't think I ever looked at one thing I was doing then. I try to remember how the dishes stacked in our one cupboard above the sink. I remember that—since our shower was contaminated by mildew—I cut pictures out of magazines and pasted them up over the foul-smelling stuff— all I can remember was some zoot-suiter and the printed phrase *The Zip Gun Boys on a Caper*! I remember that our mattress and box springs were right down on the floor, and hordes of mice thundered past our heads in the night; that I had a nightmare, when Aurora was no more than two, in which my father, then still very much alive, appeared to me under a theater marquee and said solemnly, ''Make no mistake about it: We're all dead.''

Oh! I was lonely! There were nights at home when I'd have my baby on my knees and I'd look at the poor man I was married to and feel misery far beyond anything I've known before or since. And on Thursday nights I'd come home in despair, not knowing why, just knowing it would be five days until I could go back to school.

As I remember, I wore pants and my husband's sweaters, and saddle shoes, and my hair cut like a boy's. Never any makeup. How could a sullen housewife who insisted on reading Susanne K. Langer while her cute bare-chested husband and his bare-chested friends conducted a free-for-all four-hour fight with water pistols all through the house wear makeup? But Lorna wore a mask of it. She was tall and thin and very old, twenty-four to my twenty-one. Her black hair was dyed, her curls were artificial, she wore cinch belts and high-heeled shoes and stockings.

She had been married before, to a man she didn't like, and was married now again, to a man she didn't like. And she was in sociology with me, and didn't like it, and she hated semantics. She hated reading Susanne K. Langer and asked me shamelessly for pertinent facts before each test. Lorna was in American literature with me, managed to read all the books, insisted we sit up in the front row for that one. Lorna dressed in the brightest greens and reds, not like a coed, not like a beatnik, not like a poor person or a rich person either, always wearing sharkskin or gabardine. But despite our differences of style and language and taste, and walking, even—I say—walking, because, how, without walking or singing, might we ever be "joined at the hip"? —she picked me out. I know now that she must have been as lonely as I and saw in me a disciple.

In the flimsy new cafeteria of this awful little street-corner college that was the center of my life then, that skinny lady, dressed in a kelly green sharkskin suit with a nylon blouse and stockings, sat down across from me and pulled back her red lips in a snarl. There was lipstick on her teeth. She held up jeweled harlequin glasses to her nose and peered down at her tray. "I hate fucking chocolate pudding!" she said. "I *hate* fucking chocolate cake!"

I wanted to ask her why those were the only two items on her tray but I was too afraid.

"Aren't you in semantics? I hate that fucking class!"

I had never said that word in my life and had heard it only once or twice.

"Yes," I whispered. "I do too."

Soon I'd try to take the 7:30 A.M. bus on those two precious days, so that I'd have fifteen extra minutes in the morning to have coffee with Lorna. She ate junk food, she stayed thin, and she hated *everything:* her husband, her stepchildren, every class. She was frantic with rage. Every morning when we saw each other she'd say, "You know what he did *last* night? He brought home a magnifying glass to put in front of the television set. And do you know what? His *mother's* coming out here to visit, from *Pittsburgh*, for two weeks.''

She mimicked every teacher cruelly, and the American literature man, a veteran of World War II, running to fat now, and certainly not a man of deep intelligence, who thought—or said—that Ernest Hemingway was ''the closest any human being could ever come to God,'' came in for her special attention. ''When you read a book,'' this poor devil might say, ''and things appear to be one way and actually they turn out to be another way, well, that's the difference between appearance and reality.''

''My *butt!*'' Lorna would whisper to me, or when she was really upset, ''His *dick!*''

But then there came a day when that man (who also wore gabardine, who probably had never been handsome but who carried concealed beneath his wash-and-wear shirt a heart that did more than simply beat) came into our little class of urban losers with a stack of six books, all the same, and all his. *Love Between Friends,* or *Friendship and Lovers,* or *Love in the Afternoon,* its paper cover garish, you could tell from looking that no one would buy it, but a light shone from his face that was beatific. ''My book,'' he said, in his own heaven. ''It just came in the mail. Isn't it beautiful?''

''My butt!'' I heard whispered again in my ear, but then Lorna did something amazing. In those days we wore straight skirts so tight that our buttocks were cupped in them, and we kept our legs religiously crossed while we sat, because although those skirts were calf-length the very *narrowness* of them made them hike, take walks up our legs, and the best you could hope for was to keep them pulled down over your kneecaps. A constant preoccupation, that little self-conscious tug, left hand to right knee.

Lorna uncrossed her knees. I'd seen my mother do it, on summer days, when we were alone in the car and she was driving. But, get serious! This was in class, and we were, as always, at Lorna's insistence, in the front row. Her harlequin glasses were safely in her purse. The notes she was taking now were useless hieroglyphics, she couldn't see the page. It was a hot day. I caught the smell that television used to chide us for: It came through veils of nylon and gabardine; it fought with the scent of new detergents; it joined forces with Prince Machabelli; it was the smell of cunt, pure and simple, and if *I* caught it, trying with all my mind not to, well, what did it do to that dim American novelist caught in an up-draft in that un-airconditioned quonset hut?

That night, when I went home—washed out cloth diapers on the sink in a portable washing machine my step-mother had bought me for twelve dollars, as I made creamed tuna on toast, with my baby slung on my hip like a piece of hand luggage—the world grudgingly opened up for me. If you could do that, if you could, literally, throw caution to the winds, why, then, anything was possible.

Soon, through short ribs and lamb shanks, through re-lentless green-brown-and-white dinners that put my poor husband into a stupor; through ironing and washing; lying under him with my legs spread like a damn fool and my feet pointing all the way backward to the 76 gas station on the street below—I smiled, as the mice carried on their exciting lives beneath my head. There was a way out. There might be a way out for me.

And soon I'd take an even earlier bus, leaving poor Jack to clean up the baby before he could begin to paint, and Lorna would meet me on the vacant lot we called a cam-pus, standing at the top of a short flight of cement stairs that led, as yet, to nowhere.

"So, can you guess what he did *last* night? He found an old piece of screen and told me he was going to *strain* every inch of dirt in the garden!" And I would answer, "Do you know what *he* says he's going to do now? He *says* he wants to paint aborigines in Australia, not the regular kind but the kind that live in trees and never come down, and draw them before they become completely *extinct!*''

''Oh, you are *kidding!*''

And we'd sit through sociology, and we'd giggle through semantics, and then we'd hit American lit.

They often said later that our class, or generation, was full of people who ''came from nothing.'' There was La Monte Young, who went from a seedy little saxophone player who drenched himself in cologne and made a cult of not wearing socks because he didn't *have* any socks, to what he was twenty years later, the ''father of the avant garde,'' with that long grey beard and his hair in a knot and Indian clothes and a gold American Express card, and he *still* didn't have any socks. Or the man who cashed in on Gerry Mulligan to start Pacific Records, and Gerry Mulligan also lived to be an old guy, and that record business remained. Or there was Lorna. Or me! But what the people from the ''East'' never saw, or felt, is that when you ''came from nothing,'' that there really *was* nothing back there, only a limbo of unbaptized children. When we were in the act of becoming ourselves, we did it from somewhere further back than scratch.

Lorna came from nothing. Here's what she could do. When you came to school with a cold and your nose was all stopped up, she'd lay two fingers, index and third, their nails painted brightly, on either side of your poor plugged orifice, and smile. She'd give your head a little *knock* with her other hand—I suppose she still does that, with the crisp edges of her nails, not with the brutish heel of the hand the way lower-class evangelists bully you into health—no, she'd snap her nails against the bone above your eyes. Half the time nothing would happen; we didn't really expect it to. But once there was a young man named David Mandlebaum (you may have seen him twenty years later on local television; he turned out to be the ''spokes-

man for independent taxi drivers in Los Angeles''), and
he'd had a cold for close to a week. We'd hear him sniff
in semantics, apologetically, and see him dab at his upper
lip with the fringed ends of a dirty wool scarf . . .

Lorna had no patience, and on a cold Friday morning
as we waited in the windy alleys between huts for an eight
o'clock class to be over so the nine o'clock one could
begin, David came up, snuffed and smiled, pathetically.
Quicker than the eye could really see, Lorna's fingers
danced a quick tattoo across the bones in his face and then
"Ugh," she said, and drew her hand away with what must
have been a full cup of pale snot. "Have a heart, willya?''
She dashed it out into the air and it hung there for a green
instant, then fell into the new thin grass. She ran her hand
against his dangling scarf and bony chest in what the
unobservant might have seen as a means to dry her hand,
but I was wrong.

"Ah!" the poor guy grunted. "Ah!" His face turned
pink, he buckled as if he'd been shot, and disappeared
around the corner of the hut, where we could hear him
retch, coughing his lungs clear.

"Creep," Lorna said.

There were people around us, other students, mostly
white in those days, poorly dressed and raw-boned, all
resolutely not noticing.

When David came back his face was pale and his eyes
were wide. He didn't look at us, but I happened to sit next
to him as Dr. Amneus led the class in an uninteresting
discussion of Susanne K. Langer, which I had trouble following because I got hung up on listening to the gusts of
air whistling through David's purified echoing nostrils and
down into his raw and scoured chest.

Lorna never said a word about any of that. No, it was
mostly a standard rant-'n'-rave about Harry or Harold, or
whatever his name was, and his two children from a previous marriage, and how Harold's idea about their new car

didn't coincide with *hers*. And then we'd watch as the American lit professor, large and shuffling, blushing pink, would shamble up to our little group of raffish undergraduates, so *bad* his thoughts were, it was as if he was wearing his dick straight up between his ears. He'd walk Lorna off a few steps to whisper to her and he'd cancel classes for the rest of the day.

I knew Lorna's husband was a contractor and that he'd been making a lot of money. I knew they lived in the suburb of Sierra Madre. I didn't know where that was, and didn't like to ask. But finally, when we were both seniors, and all my relatives by now chorusing that I was neglecting Aurora, and poor Jack was getting more slope-shouldered and sullen, Lorna pulled herself together and asked Jack and me to dinner.

We drove off with the baby across Glendale, Eagle Rock, Pasadena, and up into rough, scrubby hills, where Harry or Harold had built his new palace for Lorna; pale green stucco with sprinklers on the roof to ward off unruly brush fires, and palm trees, enormous, still in wooden casings, bought full-grown from the nursery but not yet planted, and interior courtyards with succulents and white gravel, and lanais where grapes were still struggling to get a grip, and plugs next to the regular electric plugs where the vacuum cleaner cord went, because the whole damn *house* was one big vacuum cleaner.

Apple green and cerise were the predominant colors in this domestic contraption that seemed to us as big as San Bernardino. I believe the living room had *three* dark green couches, and a low coffee table of vulgar blond wood, with more blond wood in the dining room, and on the walls those weird swatches of wallpaper you sometimes used to see in Italian restaurants: columns from Rome or Naples, with the Mediterranean in waves going off to the far corners of the room, and a couple of tiny human figures in Roman togas determinedly walking their way up the wall . . .

"Ah, some view," Harold kept saying to us, waving his arm at the "picture" window which took up one whole western wall, and revealed to us an entire valley below, but Jack and I couldn't take our eyes off the wallpaper mountains—in cerise and apple green. Dinner was not memorable, and Lorna looked older than usual as she did a kind of Pat Nixon imitation, thin, waspish, discontented, and fed us things like deep fried salmon cakes and Jell-O molds.

The kids from Harold's previous marriage cleared the table, shrugging self-consciously against all comments about how helpful they were. As Lorna thrummed her nails against the blond wood table, we heard, in the far-away kitchen, childish voices raised in threat and complaint. Then after some minutes, a scream, a hideous scream, and the younger one, an unattractive little girl, appeared in the doorway.

"He . . . he threw grease at me!"

Behind her, the inevitable, "Did not, did *not!* She spilled it on herself, the dumb . . ."

Lorna jumped from her chair, which tumbled noiselessly back into apple green carpet. "I told you," she hissed at luckless Harold, "haven't I told you, I've had about *enough!?*" She grabbed the girl, whose bare arm was already raising in blisters, and pushed her at a dogtrot in front of her to where we knew the guest bathroom was.

"Should I call the doctor?" my husband asked. "An ambulance or something?"

But Harold put up his hand, warning.

We heard Lorna's voice, "Now we're going to have a *talk,*" just the threatening parent-child rhetoric I'd grown up with, and then silence. And silence. The brother fidgeted in the doorway.

Five minutes later, Lorna returned, brutally pushing her

stepdaughter along in front of her, wreathed in false smiles.

"Are we all ready for dessert? Phil, do you think you could give your sister a hand?"

Dessert was, I swear, more Jell-O. We ate in a trance as Harold raised his voice against the new automatic dishwasher, which sounded like a night in a foundry. "We thought, if we put all the appliances in the kitchen, which really is a family room, then . . ."

The house was Harold's dream come true, a mad manifestation of *Sunset* magazine as it had appeared in the late fifties, with ironing boards that fell out of shuttered closets, a walk-in pantry for preserves. Stacks of linens hid like babies in a newfangled lying-in hospital; that is, the lady of the house would strip the beds and put the sheets in a mail chute that emptied out by the laundromat—it was an old-fashioned Bendix with the round window, television screen to the wet world—then, after washing, zap into the dryer—remember how *new* all that was?—then onto the shelves, which, because of Harold's ingenuity, opened on the *other* side of the wall which just happened to be in the bedroom.

The whole house was that way. He showed it to us after dinner while Lorna lagged along behind, showing by every half-gesture that she was bored, *bored,* and when Harold admitted that, yes, he knew the house was pretty big, but they were waiting for a family of their own, that thin, tired, dissipated lady-student friend of mine allowed herself a mean little smile.

Just as Lorna had said, Harold had fashioned a crude frame out of an old window screen. He used it to sift the rocks from the dirt of his vegetable garden; he meant his soil to be as soft and pure as silk. He was one of those nice, obtuse men that turn their women into snakes, and give the rest of us a bad name.

Jack and I couldn't take it, and went home fairly early,

after Harold had put in a sample load of wash for us, and given us a carton of his own zucchini and turnips.

Poor Harold never knew what hit him—either when she stayed or when she left. He never knew what he had, probably never could figure it out; always must have wondered what to make of it when he turned up later in her homilies under the embracing term, *my former husband*—though of course that eventually took in two, maybe three of them. But Harold could tell, I'm sure, when the exemplum turned on how you couldn't expect domestic comforts, or the illusion of security, or a family—even if it's a nice one—to provide you with *agape*. Harold must have known it was he she was talking about, and when she got on the subject of turnip soufflé as an example of "an abundance of *lack*"—all the sorrow that comes from pursuing the wrong things and then getting them. I always felt sorry for Harry.

He was dumb, no getting around it, but not so dumb that he didn't know enough to keep his mouth shut that night, about his daughter's arms and part of her face, because it was never mentioned after dinner as we prowled out among the cabbages, and to my knowledge never mentioned by any of them at all.

The next morning Lorna was back at school, sitting in the early morning with her coffee at a yellow cafeteria table, bitching to me again. She was so *bored,* it was driving her nuts, she couldn't stand Harold's kids, the boy was a bed-wetter and the girl allergic to house dust; Harold had brought a coffee grinder into the house that whined like a dentist's drill, and that was the first thing she heard every morning. But I'm sure that if an archangel had floated down to Lorna in a golden cloud, and smitten her with the flat side of a wide celestial sword and said, "Attention! Poor out-of-focus housewife! Some day you and your painted nails are going to amount to something, so keep that thin waist and remember to stay out of the sun and go to the dentist and get those teeth capped!" she would have been as surprised as Harold about it all, because who could foresee the manifestation of dreams? Or television? Or all that money?

I often think about it even now, in our new world; conjure up those scenes the way Aristotle told us to: I think of the terrible old joke: How do you tell when a Jewish princess has an orgasm? When she drops her emery board! I think of Lorna in some motel room in Alhambra or El Monte, the poor southeast agricultural dregs of Los Angeles, sweating under the form of our American literature professor, staring at the ceiling, considering her thirties, *coming soon,* and with them the end of youth. Did she ever drop her emery board? Could she see the future? That she would both heal and destroy?

Yes, they kept doing it, in a motel, on hot days in Alhambra, and he fell into the category of her dumb husband. (What did they do, *really?* I'm speaking to you of the days when men did push-ups on your body and called that sex, when a scholar named Lionel Trilling wrote an essay saying that clitoral orgasms were immature and narcissistic, and vaginal orgasms were mature, and half of us believed him, because, God knows, we'd known all along we were "immature" and we'd known all along we weren't having orgasms.)

Lorna's husband had put that silly round "spectacle" on his six-inch television set. Finally, Jack and I were given a set of our own by pitying relatives. We watched Kennedy before he *was* Kennedy, giving somebody's nomination speech. We watched Oscar Levant, late at night, smoking, playing wrong notes on his piano, throwing his life away. Every night, it seemed, we saw another "experimental" atomic explosion white out our tiny screen. We drank a lot. Because even then, especially then, we could see well enough there was no future.

Two months before Jack and I were to "graduate," I started an affair. Not with the boy who wore no socks, with someone else, a blond, a brute, an Australian, a would-be filmmaker. Don't ask me why. Don't *ask* me why! Here's a reason, if you could see into the future. One night Jack and I were asked to dinner by a whole other couple. They lived in a little house in the Silver Lake district of Los Angeles—a place you never used to read about or hear about, but it was there, west of downtown, east of Hollywood, north of Inglewood, south of the San Fernando Valley, a place with no borders and little character. Those frame and stucco houses jammed up against adobe hills, those one-car garages built into the houses themselves, even the fake beam ceilings and fake Spanish tiles inset up near flat roofs, and half-dying cypress and exuberant gum trees didn't necessarily make a *place*, OK?

So, we went to dinner. Both man and wife were safely out of school, no children yet, no furniture either. Just Japanese mats and paper lanterns. We sat on mats and ate dinner off mats, Jack got drunk on those mats, and what did they serve? They served hamburger, made up with cottage cheese and pineapple, because their theme was Hawaiian. The wife—a large one, named Renatta—swayed on her mat to Hawaiian music that played on the Victrola. And two weeks later we had them at our house, where Jack bit Renatta's knees out of frustration and hostility more than lust. What did we have for dinner? Spaghetti, but it was green, and so was the salad and the sponge cake for dessert, because our theme was green.

That woman died of cancer within the decade. Could I see into the future? Was that why I looked across a ramshackle classroom and found salty blond hair and a thick neck and twenty-four-inch arms and brutish ways, and *went for it?* I remember that guy, ambitious Dirk Langley, but I don't remember Jack very well at all. And we were married five years! He hated the way I held hamburgers. Was that any reason to leave him? No. But the green dinners, and Oscar Levant, and maybe the whited-out TV screens were. I don't know, don't ask me.

I know that the idea came to me at three in the afternoon with the sun shining through cypress trees and Gerry Mulligan playing on a ten-inch record. I know that Aurora was still a tot, indifferent, placid, sitting on a secondhand red couch as I spooned plum-flavored baby food into her rosy mouth. A bite piled high. She takes it in and swallows it. Nobody's home. The tune switches to "Varsity Drag." I've just learned to listen for chord changes, but it's hard when there's no piano. I'm in my early twenties, and even though they didn't think I could do it, I've gone back to school. Jack's in art school too, but he doesn't care about it. You know what he wanted to be when we came home from Europe? He wanted to be a gardener in a nunnery! That's what he said, and what I told Lorna. You can guess what she said about that.

Lorna's home today, but I don't know, I just don't want to talk to her. Jack won't be home until six: Mondays, Wednesdays, Fridays are his days at school. A field mouse comes up along the top of the red couch. We've sprayed the couch red, with red stuff out of cans. I take a spoonful of plum-colored paste, pile it high, stick it into a rosy mouth. The baby considers, looks around the living room—the dust motes in the air, the lamb shanks, the Gerry Mulligan, the paperback Susanne K. Langer, the straw mats (of a coarser grade), the tiny house, the world situation. She holds the purple stuff within her mouth, and shoots it out on her pink corduroy chest.

I couldn't . . . And here I pause, trying to make sense of history. It's my feeling that there's no point in trying to figure out why Caspar and Alexander and John-Foster and all the other bilious, sleepy, killer, respectable fiends made mincemeat of our world unless we figure out why one harmless-seeming, totally innocuous, quite innocent-appearing, absolutely-unimportant-in-the-scheme-of-things, rosy baby checks out the dust, the jazz, the baby food, the peaceful living room and dinner on the stove, and chucks it all; spits her plums out on her chest.

That night I told Jack I was leaving him, I cried, but I was filled with a desperate delight! Because he'd never bought me any birthday presents! And when we'd gone to the opera in Paris as students, he'd worn a sweater and every other man there wore a tie! He'd put up wood paneling against one wall, but left a six-inch patch where you could see ivy-covered wallpaper, and he never fixed that last patch! He never took me to listen to jazz! He had his friends over all the time and they drank beer and played with water pistols all through the house!

Some time later, when I got around to getting a divorce, I sat in Reno in a drive-in movie, during the intermission between the second and third features. The Australian, a kindly man in his brutish way, had gone to find us some pizza and Cokes. My daughter, by now a quiet three-year-old, who was slated to spend the better part of the next six years of her life in the Australian's Buick back seat as we traveled the world in search of ''adventure''or ''happiness'' (or, I see now, survival, though the subject never came up), looked at me in the gloom.

''Is there another movie?'' she asked.

''Yes, there is,'' I said with false cheer. ''This is a *triple* feature. Isn't that fun? Usually we only get to see a double feature!''

She looked at me in despair. ''Aren't we ever going home? Don't we ever get to go back? Can't we ever see Daddy again?''

The door opened and the Australian burst in. ''No pizza, just hot dogs, OK? And beer for us, and a Coke . . . for you.''

She reached out, took the Coke, the meat, and huddled in the dark, out of his sight. Already we both knew he hated weeping women, and who could blame him? He had problems of his own.

She swallowed her tears, and I, mother to a child I had orphaned myself, my own fate tied up with a hardhearted stranger, considered what I had wilfully thrown away: My home. My child's happiness. My future. My reputation as a decent person. I'd been wicked, and sown heartbreak just for the hell of it. Sometimes since then, I've wanted to say to my older daughter, *if you'd just kept that plum-colored stuff in your mouth!* But then I think: *If I'd just made that stuff into smaller bites! If I hadn't been so impatient! If I'd waited to graduate!* And I know that for years Jack remembered a ceramic pig we had. Because the day Aurora and I were leaving he broke that pig—which was small and hollow—and as I, ostentatiously, regretfully, and in an ill-concealed rage, rushed around, ironing and packing, he spent the last three hours of our married life together trying to glue together the pig. *No wonder I was leaving him!* But as we sat down to our last meal together, the young artist, who had wanted nothing more out of life than to be a gardener on peaceful lawns, to be not blown up or harmed, burst into tears. "*I knew that if I could just fix this pig, then you wouldn't leave me,*" he sobbed. "And I have all the pieces, but I couldn't fix it. Because this last piece keeps dropping back into the pig . . ."

Sometimes in the years that came after that I'd tell myself that since I had no idea then or now what I was doing, I must be part of a Larger Plan.

I would tell myself that the only way out was through, and so on. But precisely because I had kicked my own world screwy with such joy, I didn't believe Caspar and Alexander and John-Foster (when they pulled long faces and said it just might be necessary to blow one half of the known world, that larger world, to smithereens) when they said they felt sorry about it.

Pretty soon I forgot what Jack looked like, or how he talked or when he was funny, or how he took naps—or even our green dinners. Forgot our boring paradise; forgot my scorched-earth policy. Part of me said it would turn out for the best. The part that remembered the doomed little girl in the back seat had trouble buying it. Maybe we were asleep? Unconscious to the Larger Plan? If I believed it for myself, I had to extend that courtesy to the "statesmen," and the generals.

4 ❧

SEPTEMBER 1981 — JANUARY 1982

IN THE EARLY EIGHTIES, YOU HAD THE SENSE THAT THERE was nothing you couldn't do in L.A. The fact that I had just turned forty and Lorna was three years older meant absolutely nothing. She had the looks and I had the money, and by some complicated set of mathematics, we liked to feel that neither of us looked a day over twenty-eight. The days—especially the long mornings when I wasn't teaching or writing or decorating a meeting—were ours. A little shy with each other at first (for after all, it had been almost a full twenty years since we'd been friends before) we explored the "fun" things to do in this basin of pleasure.

"Mother-humping, brother-fucking, distasteful little *ball*," Lorna said to that thing that you whack across nets with a racquet, and that was the end of our tennis lessons. The prim side of me considered. Did I really need a four-times married, ill-educated, presently a waitress for a friend now that I headed up the Third Women's Bank? But Lorna's patience was just as sorely tested during our first aerobics class, when—as she lithely stretched and clapped and sweated under fluorescent lights—I skulked at the back of the class, and, when it came time for the obligatory "chorus line," was the one out of thirty girls and women who could not kick my right foot in the air at the same

68

time (or on the same beat) as the others. Then I could see my new/old friend thinking: Is it really sensible, in the light of what I want to do with the rest of my life, to commit myself to a friendship with a woman who has had two failed marriages and doesn't know her left foot from her right?

There had been this feeling, since that Sunday morning we'd met again in Lion's presence, with confetti flying and people crying out their wishes and "decrees" up to the ceiling of that hotel room, that whatever we decided to do together, it ought, somehow, to be "normal," something in the open air; something on a bicycle or a sailboat (except Lorna couldn't swim and I kept falling off). But we were dead game.

I date the real beginning of our second friendship after we'd begun again at yet another socially acceptable physical activity. For a while, five years before, the whole California world had taken to roller skates—or so it had said in the slick national magazines and the *New York Times* Sunday supplement. Now, three-quarters of the skating shops had closed, but south of the towns of Santa Monica and Ocean Park, down a street called Washington, which ran headlong into a parking lot and then sand and then a fishing pier and then the sea, a last bastion of the roller-skating craze survived. There, where the beach was a mile across and dazzling white, the city had built a wide, winding cement path for bicycles. When the roller skaters came there was no place to skate except on that modest six-foot cement strip, and the ensuing arguments, accidents, riots even, were the talk of the town. The city created a special squadron of beach police with tee shirts, Bermuda shorts, and billy clubs to create order. And so, one sunny morning, against this civic unrest, Lorna and I met for perhaps our seventh time, to try another sport. We rented skates, bent and laced them, and sailed out on to the sidewalk, holding nervously to ourselves, lamp posts, each other.

"This is shit," Lorna said. "This is harder than skating on a *rug*, for Christ's sake!" But she was smiling.

Winos lurched out of bars, hookey-playing frat boys left their beers to watch our progress, and finally an impossibly unhealthy drunk left the safety of the stucco wall where he'd been glued, to come out and give us some advice: "Look, girls! It's a perfectly natural motion."

A *natural motion*! What a concept! Lion was right. Every time you thought you'd got it down pat that you didn't, no you didn't, really have to *work* at things, you found that you had to learn it all over. The gravel in the parking lot was like running up hill in sand dunes, and then, in one wonderful instant, we were on the bike path and skimming. The off-shore breeze dried our sweat and frizzed our hair: I looked over at Lorna, and her (slightly lined) face showed pure joy.

We didn't trust ourselves to speak. We skated north, past blacks with bongos (why weren't they out somewhere being gainfully employed?), and, after we labored up a small hill, we came across a group of ten or so young men on skates who'd set up beer cans and slalomed wildly through them, while we plodded steadily by. "Later," Lorna gasped. "Later, we'll show 'em." We wheeled along as far as the deserted hotel where the heroin addicts used to stay, and then turned back.

Then a cop rolled up.

"Officer," Lorna said, "isn't it true that this is the shortest point home, I mean to Washington Boulevard? I wonder if . . ." And in a minute we had a double cop escort, sweet killers in tee shirts with peace doves on them, grasping our elbows like skaters of old on the icy Danube, telling us to *watch our step!* at every crack, and soon we were back at the low-life roller skate place, saying goodbye to our escorts like coy sorority girls, except Lorna couldn't resist tapping her cop, tracing a mole under his shirt with one sharp nail, saying, "You'd better get that taken care of, and don't let them cut it out. Be sure! Make them burn it off. It won't hurt.''

''Yes ma'am.''

''Don't put it off! And thanks for not giving us a ticket.''

Our legs felt like wings when we took off those wheels, and we wanted to celebrate in the carbonated air. We put on wrap-around skirts and walked across the bridges of the Venice canals until we found a Thai restaurant. A tiny Thai man seated us at a ''private'' table and pulled the beaded curtain. We were alone in the candle-lit dark, with ten spicy dishes coming to us in the next two hours. It was hard not to fall in love.

''Listen, Lorna, I want to know, what ever happened to that English professor?''

She widened her eyes.

''I know you were *doing* it, Lorna! So, tell me! What happened?''

''Well, you know, of course. I went ahead and married him.''

''You *didn't! That* guy?'' Tactless, yes, but how could she have been so dumb?

''I hated those kids of Harry's! I hated Sierra Madre or wherever the hell it was.'' Iced Thai coffee arrived and she watched the thick condensed milk sink down into the thinner black stuff. ''I just . . . Oh, hell, *you* know, Edie! I couldn't think of a way to get out, and Rance said he loved me, and Harry obviously didn't, so . . . I don't know. I just did it.''

''What did Rance do with *his* wife? Didn't he have a wife?''

''Christ. It was so embarrassing. He didn't have any money because he worked at that pathetic school, and he had two kids of his *own* and his wife never even raised her voice at him, and she wouldn't take anything of hers out of the house. The books especially. They were all out in a garage in that crappy place they lived, *Alhambra*, for

God's sake, so I never had a place to keep my car, and I had to do all this heavy-duty housekeeping, because that wife adored him so much she let him keep the boys. They *hated* me, until the younger one saw me going down on his dad when he came home from school, and he got the idea *that* might be fun . . .''

"But how . . . I'm sorry . . . how . . .''

She laughed. "How could I *do it*? I really believed in that literature stuff! I really thought you could *think* your way out of a bind! I thought Rance knew something! When he brought in those copies of his novel that day . . .'' As though she could read my mind, which of course she could, Lorna went on. "I could see stuff in his novels. I saw where he wanted to be. *He* didn't want to be stuck in a two-bedroom house in Alhambra! He didn't want his first wife or those kids or *me* either! But he didn't have the . . . he didn't have the . . .''

"Energy? Stamina? Talent?"

"He was just a slash hound.''

"So?''

"So when I left him after *seven years,* his wife moved right back in. They didn't even have to change around the furniture.''

Husband number three had been a Jamaican musician named Prince Le Boeuf who dressed all in white. He too had been great in the sack, at first, but liked, Lorna found out, to bugger his gentleman friends—all in the spirit of fun. Lorna found out there were limits to her tolerance: "I told him, bugger *me*! I've got an asshole like everyone else in this great democracy! I'll speak in a deep voice, you shut your eyes, and who'll know the difference?'' He took her at her word, she said, for several long years, and indeed—on a night when he'd decided to go straight for the sheer variety of it—she conceived her one and only child, born in 1972, a lovely coffee shade, dear Letty ("Because of that tune they used to play on the old Haw-

thorne show—'Because I'll miss you, so long, so long,
Letty, doo de doo de doo' '').

We'd begun on white wine; Lorna's eyes were sad. "I
never had anything, you know," and—as I raised my hands
in protest—"I wasn't smart like you. I could just barely
figure out what I didn't like, and I could see that getting
some black guy's dick stuck up me seven times a week
was ruining my looks. And I couldn't sit through a double
feature at the movies. And all his friends knew. And I had
to go to work as a bartender because he never could get
any gigs. And my hair was turning grey. And he took all
my money away as soon as I made it. So . . ."

"Well," I said, "you look wonderful now, God
knows."

"That's because of Isadore in great part," she said, and
smiled. "My fourth. He was really a pretty good guy. I
know people made fun of him because he was bald, but
he helped me get past my —well, you know. You've heard
him."

"You don't mean Dr. Isadore Israel, on KWHY? You
were married to *him*?"

"He was very nice. Really. I mean it. You know what?
Don't laugh, but he was really the one who first taught me
about tax deductions. How if you hated the government
you'd be a damn fool to march in the demonstrations. All
you'd have to do is fix it that you deducted so many ex-
penses that you'd never pay any taxes. See? It's so simple,
really. Why don't we *all* do it? Why do we let them go on
building bombs and all that stuff? If everybody in the
United States took every legal deduction they were ever
entitled to, my God! They couldn't afford to buy a *rifle* at
the Pentagon! They couldn't afford a roll of caps for a *cap*
gun!"

She'd raised her voice. I remembered that the big building next door was some kind of think tank. The restau-

rant's Asian owners sidled up to listen outside our bead curtains.

"Dr. Isadore Israel," I said. "I can't believe it. I heard him tell some woman who called in to his show that it was perfectly all right for her boy to wear pantyhose, that it was just a stage he was going through. Did you hear that show?"

"Oh . . . Izzy was all right. He was the one who finally told me that as long as there . . . that as long as I . . ." She went on to say that her life had taken its real turn when she'd fallen in with Dr. Israel: that he was the one who'd first encouraged her to take classes, not just in primal therapy and the est weekends, but in rolling and falling. All those seminars were so expensive that only professional people went, and though those California gatherings were laughed at by the dignified East, they were really only longer versions of the expense-account lunch—longer hours, looser clothes. Lorna and the good doctor even had their own seminar for a while: freedom within marriage—some such thing—until they got their own divorce.

"But he was a good guy, Isadore. And he was always nice to Letty. We really did just grow away from each other. He was too serious. He wanted me to read too much. *I* just wanted . . ." She stopped, and that preposterous talent of hers hung between us. How many husbands (and friends) had she driven away because they didn't know how to get on speaking terms with her weird gifts?

"OK," and she sighed. "What about you?"

If hers was a tale of ambition and silliness, mine was a story of ambition and fear.

"Well, you knew Jack."

"A nice person, yes."

"He turned out to be a *very good* artist!"

"But you left him, right? Isn't that right?"

I couldn't talk about Jack. Instead I confined my remarks to Dirk Langley, the bronzed man who had come
all the way up here (by way of his thumb, he said) from
the west coast of Australia, Perth, to make it as a director
of surfing movies. I "fell in love," not with Dirk's face,
or his disposition, or, God knows, his character, but with
his longitude, his latitude, his geographical safety.

And when he left L.A., to travel to Oahu's windward
coast, then back to Reno for the divorce, and down to
Manzanillo, then over to the Marquesas, then over to
Capetown, well, I packed up a kit bag, and toted along
the beautiful but terminally depressed Aurora.

"I had adventures," I told Lorna, sadly. "I've been to
the Galapagos."

"So, what happened?"

Somewhere along the line I got pregnant again, and
while he'd been aces about Aurora, sticking her in the back
seat of his sports car along with the rest of the soft luggage, Dirk couldn't bring one of his own babies into this
world. "What," he'd said, purpling with the attempt to
put a thoughtful sentence together, "What if it was a boy,
see? What would happen to it then?"

So we'd parted company and country on a winter's day
in Manhattan. I'd found a loft and learned to make a living. "The work ethic," I said lamely. "I think it caught
up with me. But Dirk's back here now. He's cashing in on
the Australian movie craze. To his surprise and mine."

"I'll never work. At a *real* job, I mean. I know it."

"So . . . how do you live? And, aren't you . . . uh . . ."

But the time had come for Lorna to speak of Lion Boyce;
the love of her life, her prophet, her reason for being, her
inspiration, her fun.

It was Lion who taught Lorna to sky dive, Lion who
suggested she go beyond rolling and falling into aikido;
Lion who got her to where she could weigh two hundred
pounds or more, and down to twenty. She could never

break through that and actually levitate—although he insisted it could be done. Lion who got her to move an (empty) salt shaker a quarter of an inch by staring at it, Lion who taught her that you almost always won a wrestling match if you lined your underwear with hundred-dollar bills.

"What it really is, kid," she said, her eyes and teeth shining like a bobcat's, "is that I know Harry loved me, but I couldn't *stand* him; and I know Rance loved me, but finally you can even get tired of oral sex, you know? I don't think Isadore ever loved me, I was just some ditz he could turn into something better, and I tried, but I couldn't say I really loved him; and Prince, well, he isn't worth talking about, the best thing about him was his white pointy shoes; and the universe knows that Lion Boyce doesn't love anybody, there's a whole level where I wouldn't even have him in my living room! But I love Lion, that's *it* for me. I love Letty, but Lion, he's the one I love. He's the one I really love."

We spent the rest of the afternoon behind the rattling beads, finishing off three carafes of wine and balancing them with Thai coffee, talking about men. I tried to remember Jack—his goodness—my inability to stay in his house; I pulled out a hundred pointless anecdotes about the mad Australian and my eternal disappointment at the simple fact that though he was a great traveler, he never wanted to travel where *I* did; and as for me, you could show me the inside of perfect thirty-foot "tubes" in every country with a coastline, I could have cared less. "And yet, in Lion's seminar, I kept saying I wanted to go to the beach." I was beginning to lose the thread. "Maybe I just didn't want to go to the beach with *him*. But he gave me Denise . . ." I turned a gold false wedding band around, so that diamonds, two full carats, mounted side by side, usually hidden in my palm, glittered in the perfumed candlelight. "See these? These are the material manifestation of my daughters. *Nothing* can harm them, I've seen to that, I know it!''

''That's why you met Lion, that's why the universe sent you up there,'' Lorna said solemnly. ''There's a reason for everything. Everything always turns out for you more exquisitely than you ever planned. That's what Lion says.''

IN THOSE EARLY DAYS, IF SHE TRUSTED YOU, ALL LORNA could talk about was the fun of it. She worked nights in Zucky's Deli and ''played'' all day, taking martial arts classes. She was a strict vegetarian and lived in one small room with Letty, saving her money for round-trip PSA fare up the coast to San Francisco for Lion's weekend trainings. There was much more to all that than the simple weekend that Skip and I had gone to. There were day-long ''Treasure Map'' workshops where people gathered with shoeboxes of glue and glitter and colored pencils to make pictures of what they wanted out of life: *Letty and Lorna are fully enjoying their used but perfectly running Jaguar* said one that hung prominently above their made-up daybed, and I was so into it that I was about to turn over some of the Third Women's Bank's ill-gotten Argentine money for an unsecured car loan when an old geezer who always sat in Lorna's station at Zucky's Deli up and died and left ''that nice waitress in Station 2 who always makes my arthritis feel better'' a used but perfectly running Jaguar; and that same week, Letty's teacher, who lived in a no-pets condominium, got caught sheltering a very nimble kitten and turned it over to Let. Naturally, they named it Jag.

There were all-day courage games, to get over your fear of rejection, and all-day skydivings, ''to get a sense of the *confront* between you and the universe!'' But the best times, Lorna said, were the forty-eight-hour games of ''Commando''—Lion's personal favorite. Forty or fifty of

Lion's closest assistants, Lorna included, would split up and declare four square miles of Sausalito *war country*! The object would be to steal a grandfather clock, or a fetus in a bottle, or a five-pound hunk of hashish; and they used all their skills to do it—the blue team and the orange team. The booty could be in someone's house or stuck in a tree; but usually Lion rented a boat out on the bay. He'd seen movies as a child where people breathed through reeds, and he was crazy about the idea.

"Listen," Lorna told me repeatedly, "you've got to come up and at least look. Because you've never seen such fun in your entire life. And, *listen*! I know there's money in it. You could get Lion to franchise it all across the nation!"

Such was Lion's influence even on our lives, that Skip and I flew north for yet another weekend to "observe" a game of Commando. We were handsomely provided for on a Sausalito mole next to the yacht in question, supplied with down sleeping bags, a picnic basket, and a case of Schramsberg.

The trouble was there was nothing much *to* see. All we could perceive was the yacht, peacefully bobbing in the San Francisco bay under cool grey skies. Every once in a while you'd spy two inches of pipe from a lonely snorkler just breaking the surface of the grey bay, but then it would disappear with a subdued gurgle. Or you'd get a strong smell of jasmine or curry. The action was always behind you. You'd hear a giggle, a creak of boards on the dock, and perhaps once an hour a young man or woman would *appear*, laughing and swearing, coated in white flour, his or her cover blown, because flour was their weapon. Once you were made visible with white, you were out of the game.

The night was a little more exciting, punctuated by quick flares and muted explosions and sky divers in black para-chutes and occasional hired helicopters zipping past; and all manner of dwarfs and toddlers and doggies and nurses and nuns and *nobody*. It was—as Lorna had repeatedly told us—simply the applications of skill, in which human ladders could be erected up to twenty or thirty feet because all the people on the top rungs weighed less than twenty pounds. The smells that made you turn around were made by Lion's devotees who were studying to be perfume swamis, and if those human ladders from the orange team trying precariously to scale the swaying yacht from an almost invisible inflatable dingy happened to crumble, it was most probably because a cadre of hotshots on the blue team were thinking hard from the opposite side of the yacht, *You're weak, you're weak, you're noodle weak, you silly little babies*! And the man at the bottom of the ladder would concentrate, concentrate, but then his knees would buckle, the dingy would squirt from under him and that would be that.

The reason Skip and I—even though we knew what they were up to—couldn't see much was because, Lorna assured me later, "invisibility" was what they worked on the most. When, safely back in L.A., I told her she *couldn't* be invisible, she wouldn't let up on me for several weeks, arranging to meet me on crowded corners where I wouldn't be able to find her, making me wait, and then reporting to me everything I had done while I was waiting. Then she would tell me that the opposite of being invisible was to be in two places at once, and I don't know if it was the suggestion or what but I saw people that looked like Lorna all over the place for a couple of weeks, and then just tried to forget it.

But Skip told Lorna kindly that any question of franchising was simply out of the question. "You know, and certainly Edith and I know, that a great deal of good can come out of these weekends," he said to her. "But in situations of this kind you simply must have something to franchise and someone to run it after you've set it up. You must have a product, my dear. I'm sorry to be old-fashioned about it, but there it is. Even a brothel must have real women in it, and I'm afraid the idea of fun is more intangible—more suspect, even—than sex.''

Lorna shot me a scornful glance, but I had to agree with him. It had been hard enough getting people to stay in Lion's original seminars. It wasn't just that they didn't trust him but that they hated what he was talking about. Pay a couple of hundred dollars to have two days of *fun* and learn the secrets of the universe? Well, *hell*, they could go to the beach for nothing and take in a flick for ten bucks. Besides, the decade had turned; it was the eighties, and consciousness-raising was out of style.

Lion spent a little less than two years of batting around northern and southern California, teaching people how to laugh, to triple their wealth, to get what they wanted by lighting vanilla candles. Then, after turning on no more than maybe five thousand enthusiastic souls, Lion suddenly took a trip to the pyramids, which—when he came back—he said had changed his life. He said he was quitting the seminar business in order to learn to materialize wristwatches.

THE REAL STORY CAME TO LIGHT A FEW MONTHS LATER. After Lion had left, he'd formed another corporation, consisting of himself and maybe two dozen of his best commandos. Those guys, all in their middle twenties and absolutely *up* for getting rich, went into the drug-smuggling business. So when Lion took TransWorld Airlines over to that pleasant Indian ashram to visit the then still-living Baba Muktananda, the young pilgrim took advantage of the opportunity to load up with opium, hash, cocaine. Being mostly invisible, he and his buddies, smiling, wearing conservative suits, clothed in energy blankets of dazzling light, flew plastic vials of contraband back into

Switzerland, hidden in bottles of bright pink Indian pome-
granate juice. A phalanx of his devoted girls—slightly
bruised from rolling and falling, dizzy from conjuring
Chanel 19 out of their left palms and matching it exactly
to the ''real'' perfume they'd spritzed on their right, would
be waiting for the boys at the airport.

They'd rent a chalet for a week or so of skiing and
making love. They'd rise at dawn for icy dips in Lake
Geneva, and there are those who swear they saw Lion,
stark naked and bright pink, ''ski'' up the side of the
broad, squat fountains dotting that dignified lake. Maybe
if they'd spent some of their time making invisible ladders
outside the palaces that housed the disarmament talks, we'd
be in a different place today. Be that as it may, they did
aikido bounds, generated heat to melt circles in the snow,
and leapt neatly out, without disturbing the icy crust.
Then, dressed up as the ''swim team from San Marino,''
they'd whistle half a million dollars worth of drugs across
the North Atlantic and into Newfoundland, catch a ferry
south, past Nova Scotia, and right on in under the Statue
of Liberty's chipping nose, because, these young commandos reasoned, who'd ever suspect anyone of bringing
in dangerous drugs from *Newfoundland*?

Perhaps it was the fact that tough-spirited New York was
the final drop, but they got caught upstate on their third
trip, near Saranac Lake, as they began their loop ''home.''
While all those dumb and pretty girls went into their dumb
act (why did it take a punk like Lion to show us so definitively that it's *all* an act, all of it, every breath that any
of us takes, so, since that's what it is, let's make it a *good*
act?), while they, as I say, went into their dumb act and
managed to get off on the grounds of having been duped,
Lion and his few trusted male associates were thrown into
a cold, hard Buffalo, New York slammer, where—within
two weeks—they escaped in the soft clammy fragrance of
a garbage truck. When they were finally discovered, lay-

ered in shelves of rotting vegetables, Lion dazzled himself and all by being in two places at once so convincingly that his ''invisible'' associate escaped again.

Of course, again, they caught him. The cops were really mad at this dope-running pipsqueak and took him to a room with one small window to think over his crimes until the morrow; not even a shower for *him*! I do like to think of Lion (real name, Hugh) then, with his slightly bucked teeth, white milky skin, and those vacant blue eyes of the Irish lower class—that's where he came from, just like me—crouched in a corner, shivering, his usually fastidious get-up encrusted in gore. And I know, because of his soft good looks, no matter how strong his will, he would have been raped a few times in his first hour during any jail stay, and so, violated, sick, humiliated, and caught, Lion disappeared.

''Baba, help me *now*,'' he must have said, and Baba— though when he later came to Los Angeles would give antidope sermons to the multitudes—must have come through for that plucky little psychopath. Lion vaporized through solid walls, vamoosed into the air.

The cops were between a rock and a hard place, as they say, and the stories from that time show it. What was worse? Admitting that one lonely guy escaped *for the second time* from a cold stone jail or admitting to what ninety-nine percent of the folks thought of as the alternative (if they thought about it at all), that the pol-eece done stove in his skull, and clapped him back in the garbage truck, only dead this time? Lion's mom even turned up to bewail, and threaten to sue, and give a news conference to which almost nobody came, though I clipped her photo from the *Daily News*. ''They murdered my poor Hughie,'' she wailed, and everyone who knew him began to believe that Lion really was dead, except damned if you wouldn't reach up to scratch your nose and find your hand drenched in the smell of Brut (which was what he'd taken into the pyramids with him to block out the stench of five thousand years of Egyptian piss). Or you'd go to your car, and there'd be a three-foot white silk scarf draped across the steering wheel; or you'd be crashed out on the couch, watching TV with the family, beat after the day's work, not thinking of anything, and you'd feel *less* of the couch underneath you . . .

But by that time none of Lion's old fans wanted him around anyway, because their feelings were hurt. Those few thousand people whose money he'd taken—and given them much more than their money's worth, be it said— were Christians and Jews, mostly. They had it in their minds that all this radiance—oh, he was a bug on that particular word, that particular concept—was to help you be *good*. If you learned to project a jolt of energy out of your fingertips that might be measured in tests of simple physical strength, or make "money come back to you," or heal the sick, or pass an exam, that was—it *had* to be— a virtue as well as an accomplishment. It existed to make you a "better" person. If not, weren't we to be counted among the damned?

There were those who felt shocked, swindled, ripped off in their minds. They began to consider whether in fact that funny-as-a-crutch little charlatan hadn't set up the seminars in the first place with a *foul purpose* in mind, recruiting disciples only to persuade them into a life of crime. It was whispered about that Lion was the Devil incarnate and that those who had laughed with him had given him their souls.

But I get ahead of myself. All we knew when he left L.A. was that Lion had it in his mind to materialize those wristwatches. *"Why,"* Lorna asked me, in more anguish than she'd ever displayed over any of her four husbands, "can't the bastard go out and buy a *Timex*? My God! He's such a *slit*! You know what he does when he stays at your house when he's in town? You have to buy him ten pounds of bananas! You have to press his suits! You have to rub his back! You . . .''

I never asked if she'd slept with him. I imagined so, but I knew it wasn't the sex she missed but the fun, the costumes, and roller skates. She missed those commando raids! Meeting at midnight in a sleeping San Francisco suburb, *making the plan* with people you knew so well. Tying a sash of blue or orange around your wrist or ankle, dressing in black like the Japanese assassins of old, crouching in fallen leaves at dawn, shivering, hungry, moving by baby steps to take out your opposing number on the team, scuba diving through murky water, getting tagged out by someone you knew, and only the twin bursts of bubbles in a dark bay to show you were both laughing yourselves sick underwater; or the skydiving, Lion's very favorite sport. Lorna timed her trips with his because you were perfectly safe with him, his spirit would hold you up if your chute failed.

Once when she dove with him his helmet had slipped down over his face; as she hurtled past him, squeaking with joy, the face he turned to her was plastic and blank, his energy field pulsing blue with fear. Even then she didn't worry, she said, because he was invincible.

When he left to pursue his second career, and it was clear she wasn't going to be included in his plans—whatever they appeared to be—I think she suffered her first broken heart. When I called her on the phone, she answered in a voice choked with sobs, which she tried to pass off as a cold. When he was jailed and his story sifted down to us, she was assaulted once again.

''I know what it is, that he didn't take me along,'' she said fiercely, as we skated one day. ''I was too old for him. I wasn't pretty enough. There's nothing *anyone* can do about that, you know, *nothing*. Have you looked at Jane Fonda? Beef jerky in tights! Well, fuck him! Fuck *her! I* don't give a shit!'' And when she found a white silk scarf across her front door, making that wooden rectangle a big present to her, she made me come out to the Santa Monica palisades, just five blocks west of the deli where she worked, to watch as she handed that silken swatch to an old, sad woman on a bench. "Here, take it! I don't want it any more! Put it around your throat! You know that asthma you've got? Use this, and keep your windows closed at night. You'll feel better . . ."

We tried not to lose what we had. We continued to go about town "having fun," and when Baba Muktananda himself blew into Santa Monica, camping out in an enormous fiberglass "tent" for about a year, we went down there once a week, knowing that Lion had styled himself Baba's devoté. By now we were well within the mainstream. The place was always packed with movie stars and financiers and warmongers from the Rand Corporation who worked directly across the street. The custom was to chant in the dark for an hour. Then the lights went up and the congregation formed into a mile-long convoluted line, waiting to bow before the guru and get whopped by his peacock feather. The people I nodded to while waiting in line there, well, I may not have helped my spiritual life much, but I brought more good clients to the bank.

You had to bring an offering of fruit to get smacked by the feather, and one afternoon I noticed Lorna was empty-handed.

"You don't have a fruit!" I said, and was as scandalized as when my kids forgot their gym clothes, but she just shrugged, and held up her fingers, testing the wind. "He's got good energy," she said. "You absolutely have to give him that. Do you feel it on your skin?"

I did, but it only made me sad. It was what you'd get in those second-rate hotel rooms of Lion's, and there you could watch the hair on your forearms rise up, and you'd know you were in for a forty-eight-hour party, but here it was just ozone in the air.

Up at the front of the crowded room, banked up against a throne both makeshift and ornate, a flock of American adolescents in saffron robes directed the religious traffic, controlling the double line of pilgrims, tossing offered fruit into baskets, pushing the faithful forward and to their knees, before moving them on.

They took my pineapple, pitched it into a wicker basket where it would be carried next door to their temporary restaurant to make up some of the most unappetizing vegetarian fare I'd ever seen, and then I knelt before the visiting celebrity Indian.

"Give me power!" I prayed with all my might. "Let my children live to be a hundred! And, me too, of course." I looked up, he winked, smiled, and whooshed me with his feather.

Then I moved off to the left and watched the shaven boys and girls in orange when they saw the empty-handed waitress.

"It is not . . ." or "You cannot . . ." I don't know what I heard, but I saw Lorna Israel, in her deli uniform, step forward. She didn't kneel, but smiled at the youthful-seeming Baba. He put both hands on the arms of his chair. His disciples, seeing his intention, helped him up. The Indian and the waitress stood for a fraction of a second, in half-embrace. He dropped his feather, drew both his hands along her cheeks, leaving gleaming trails of stars (which she explained away at work as frostbite from a skiing trip to Mammoth). Straight up, she put her own palm straight over his heart. He grinned. She squared her shoulders. The place smelled funny, as if lightning had struck, and then it was over.

Lorna had to work that night, and I had a meeting next morning at eleven. I dropped her off at the deli and then drove home. We were supposed to jog the next day; this time I swore I would talk.

I'd never had the nerve, during the days when Lion got

caught, then escaped, got caught then, escaped again, to say, "Look, Lorna, didn't you hang out with that darling maniac just to keep from doing the stuff that *you* really ought to be doing?" It's true that behind her back Lion had spoken of Lorna rather meanly as "my antibiotic"; true, too, that Lorna, since the revival of our friendship, without appearing to really be doing much of anything, had come over a couple of nights a week—simply as a visiting single woman without a date—when Denise had badly sprained her ankle at the local shopping mall's skating rink. Lorna had sat on our couch watching prime-time television with her hand draped across the ace bandage, and Denise had been out of it in one week. A truly remarkable recovery, the doctor said.

But Lorna had always been mean, and sharp, and even in her new-found radiance, grumpy, and given to malicious remarks and impatient; not terribly easy to get along with—in other words, not very *good*. It seemed neither right nor true that she might have power, supernatural power, that she might be a prophet or minor messiah; that she might have the power to heal. She was a lady like me who snapped at her daughter in the close quarters of a Bullock's dressing room. Beyond that, her face was beginning to fall.

The next morning, when we'd jogged—or walked—a mile and sat down on that bench on the cliffs looking out over the ocean, she once again worked herself up into a tizzy. "It wasn't as if I didn't go out of my way for him. It wasn't as if there was a *task too small* for me to undertake!"

I was listening as hard as I could, but damned if I could hear if it was *him* or *them* she was saying. "Did they care, any of them, what I did or thought—what I *was*! Fuck, no! I was somebody to screw, or do errands, and now I'm . . ."

But she stopped short at saying she was too old. "Now

I'm not going to *do* it anymore. Now I'm going to do what
I want to do!''

IN THE NEXT FEW WEEKS I HAD TO WORK, REALLY WORK,
for a change. There were investors who, for the first time,
balked at putting their money in our bank. I was ready to
take it personally, but Skip, always the kindest of men,
reassured me. ''It's not you, dearheart. It's the world situation, that's all. You've got to remember, these are very
conservative men. They want to be able to tell their own
investors—with conviction—that their money is safe.''

So we worked, and made presentations, and found safe
places to put our own money, once we got it. Within five
months, we'd tripled our base again, and I didn't get a
chance to see Lorna once.

Until one Sunday morning. Aurora had come home that
Saturday night, late, with three others from a double date.
They'd stayed up all night, gone out on the balcony to see
the sun rise, smoked a little dope, which I whiffed through
our own open windows as the sun, somewhere, began to
think about rising. It was a perfect Canyon morning, silver
grey and cool, and some owls who didn't know enough to
call it a night kept on hooting. I could hear that, and Skip's
soft breathing, and saw an Audubon warbler sail past and
perch on the eucalyptus outside our window. Ground fog
in the canyon depths and a pearl sky above. It couldn't
have been better. Downstairs I heard Aurora and her
friends conversing in furtive, cozy whispers.

They'd turned on the television, very low—or had had
it on all night, who knows—when, at six A.M. sharp, I
heard Aurora's ladylike voice raised in a siren scream:
''Mom! *Mom*! Come down and look at this!''

I jumped up, ran downstairs, and there, in the dawn,
was Lorna, looking ten pounds lighter and twenty years

younger, wearing a linen blazer, her hair in sun-red curls, grinning from ear to ear.

"Don't let them tell you life is suffering," she said, and I heard it as if from Lion himself. "That's a crock. Life is a gift, a present from God to us, and don't you be *rude* about it, OK? You are the master of your mind and life, *you* are god in action! Now I know you don't believe that, or why would you be watching *television* at six o'clock in the *morning*? But it's true!"

"Let's change the channel," one adolescent remarked, and the other two chimed in, but Aurora said, "No! Why don't you go down and get us some breakfast?"

I went over and sat down by my daughter; we didn't touch all that easily, but it seemed like we didn't have to. We heard the words, "Everything always turns out for you more exquisitely than *you* ever planned!" What if the world was more than the nightly news led us to believe? What if there was something smiling behind our universe? What if every dollar you spent really *did* come back to you vastly multiplied? "Yes, I know you don't believe me, but what have *you* got to lose? *You're* up at six in the morning, right?"

The television Lorna (now Lorna Villanelle) couldn't stop smiling, and we laughed back at her. The kids trooped up with Grape Nuts, and Aurora commanded them: "Listen to this. It's really interesting, you know?"

I called Lorna the next day and asked her out to lunch. We decided to go to Michael's, that lovely fortress of the rich. Several nice things happened that day that went beyond the pleasure of us seeing each other again. "What I'd like," Lorna said once we were seated, "is to make a ten-minute video tape and show it to all young wives everywhere in all their little houses, and say to them, 'Don't give up! Because, look, we . . .' "

"We once were just as you," I finished for her. I was dressed in grey silk. I wore rings on every finger just for the hell of it. She wore kelly green linen, and her fingers, too, drooped with jewels. We ordered champagne, a soufflé, fresh berries. We were treated as royalty because when we'd come in Lorna'd given the maître d' a hundred. "There's nothing harder than to be a waitress, or a maître d'," she'd said.

We laughed, and talked, and tried to hold on to it, amazed that our pretend jobs had turned into something real. I want to reassure everyone that sometimes things turned out well in those days, and I know they will again—well, they *are* again!

There was a cloud of negative energy in the restaurant at the best table, and Lorna asked the waiter what or who it was. "Why, honey, that's our Secretary of State!"

Lorna wanted to see if she could make him impotent, but I told her no. "We could do it if we worked together!" But I said we had our investments to think of, and we concentrated on getting him to spill his glass of ice water instead. It was easy!

A prescient universe had allowed the restaurant to be visited by many celebrities that day, including our two un-favorite ex-husbands: Dirk Langley, now directing a new Australian movie that wasn't taking off quite the way it should, and Prince Le Boeuf, the Jamaican musician, trying mightily to fill the late Bob Marley's shoes. They were both troopers that day, coming over and shaking hands, and raining kisses on us all around before they returned to their tables. We appreciated it and gave them full marks.

But when George Christy from the *Hollywood Reporter* came in, he zipped over to *our* table, because already he was a Lorna Villanelle fan, and he knew friends who trusted their money to my bank. His photographer took *our* picture, to the curiosity—and envy—of the other lunching ladies.

The Secretary of State sulked. We, in turn, waved and

smiled and directed George and his camera to two other tables, Dirk Langley—''Such a brilliant man!'' and ''Prince Le Boeuf—he's undertaking such a compassionate mission, recreating Marley!''

The lights and the camera moved away. I looked at Lorna.

''Listen,'' I said, ''sometimes my shoulder blades ache. It's not the bank and I'm very happy at home, happier than I ever thought I could be. Still, there's a place under my shoulder blades . . .''

''Your heart,'' she said, ''the other side of your heart. It's the future that's bothering you. I don't blame you either. It's . . .'' And we looked over at the best table in the house. I'm no expert, but even I could see the black air around him, like a wood stove that doesn't draw properly.

''Hold my hand,'' I said. ''I want some healing, OK?''

She took my wrist, my left one, above the bone, and pressed. We drained our champagne. Across the room they snapped pictures of Prince and Dirk, and those two bowed to us in acknowledgment from separate tables, and we bowed back. ''Every dollar you spend,'' she said.

And I answered, as the waiters tried to avoid the sight of two women holding hands, ''comes back to you vastly multiplied, and that's OK! That's OK with me!''

5

FALL 1986

WHAT IS IT ABOUT HAPPINESS THAT IMPLIES AN ENDING? Again and again, in the three, four years that followed, I had a sense of having outlived my time. It wasn't just the sense of getting old. Aurora graduated from high school, and—disdaining college for a year—had begun to work for Skip as the world's most beautiful and self-assured courier. Eleven out of every fourteen days, she traveled for the company with a briefcase of her own (sometimes handcuffed to her wrist), carrying messages we didn't want to trust to the mail. In every city she stayed in the homes of Skip's associates, a model of the new American decorum. Her Spanish improved by the minute, and the two weekends a month she stayed home we were peppered by flowers and poems and telexes from smitten Hispanic professionals. How she loved it! And how she relished reminding her hulking high school compatriots, who, most of them, had gone on immediately to UCLA or to marriage or both, "I'm an international courier!"

Denise commuted from our canyon home into a junior high school she hated in the Pacific Palisades—another of those lovely communities that have no boundaries, can scarcely be found if you don't know where they are. This one was south of Topanga, a few miles inland from the

beach, a strict and conventional middle-class paradise—
but we still kept our wilderness home.

Happiness was, for us, difficult to apprehend. Lion
Boyce had assured us repeatedly in the old days, *nothing
is too good to be true, or too good to expand in richness
and beauty*. Still, there were nights up in our canyon,
where we'd be playing Scrabble, or Skip would be fretting
because he couldn't do the *Times'* one-minute crossword
puzzle in less than forty seconds, or—more typically—
helping Denise with beginning algebra, or I'd be assuring
her that the snobby little kids in the B9 or A8 of Palisades
Junior High would sooner or later treat her with the proper
respect (though, as far as I could see, they were doing that
already), that I'd think, *Watch it*! This is too good to be
true.

A good deal of my life, and Skip's, was devoted to
acquisition, but on late evenings, as we all read, perhaps,
in the quiet living room, the muted tickertape downstairs
seemed to weave another kind of aural lace. Not money
but safety it ticked out, and the quiet that spread out around
us in the nighttime canyon said the same thing. Safety.
Was this it then—Paradise? Could be. Every Sunday, Lorna
Villanelle came on in a syndicated, midmorning time slot
and assured us that we shouldn't be nervous if we weren't
suffering, that happiness was natural; that *abundance was
our natural state*.

Most weeks we'd watch. If she was in the country, Aurora would have had a "date" the night before that she'd
have hated. "I may be beautiful but I'm not *dense*," she'd
mutter to a friend into the phone while she watched, and
Denise would drag her spending-the-night girlfriends down
from her tumbled-about bedroom: "This lady used to be
a friend of Mom's," she'd say. "We've got to watch."
And Skip might look up from a puzzle. We'd slouch
through and around the living room, still in our bathrobes,
and watch Lorna on TV as she once again explained her

chosen name, *Villanelle*, Lorna Villanelle—"It's a poem,"
she'd say, "that's at once simple and beautiful, and it re-
peats its lines, sometimes one way, sometimes another
way, but they're the same lines. So . . . I can say . . . My
universe is filled with inspiring, rewarding, creative adventures and fun, and right now, I'll be frank, it's easy
for *me* to say, because it sounds OK to me, but *you . . .*"
and here she'd look, with such earnestness tinged with her
old exasperation, that I'd shiver, remembering, "Well,
maybe you're not exactly ready for all this! Maybe you're
alone, or sick or unhappy, or, really, just bored. But if
you were to say, 'My universe is filled with romance and
excitement! I am inundated with creative adventures and
fun!' If you were to say that, to *go* for that, you'd be
having an adventure, right there. I don't care if you were
fixing dinner for a man who sifted dirt through a strainer,
you'd still *have* your adventure, in your mind!"

Aurora might raise the lashes of her lovely eyes as she
watched, while talking on the phone, Denise and her buddies get the giggles, and—if Skip and I were sitting on the
same couch, he might poke me with his bare foot. That
dirt-sifter again! Or that funky musician who could only
get pleasure if he were hurting somebody else! Or those
"intellectuals" who could only love you if you changed
for them. We knew those married stories far better than
the one about the wine at Cana. I remembered them as
though they were my own life.

When Lorna got to her anecdotes about "sin" (although
she didn't believe in sin as such, and she'd pause for five
minutes to explain to her unlearned viewers what it meant
to speak in "figurative" language), damned if she didn't
bring up attachment to meaningless material things; like
dishwashers whose noise drowned out conversation, or
wallpaper that mimicked the world but could never match
it in beauty, or that, if you were looking for the love of
God and settled for spouses who criticized you instead—

that earthly love might be roughly comparable to, say, an afternoon in Alhambra in an ancient motel that reeked of mildew, compared to the Helmsley Palace. It was not that you were locked *out* of happiness, quite the opposite, but that you shouldn't settle for less than celestial double rooms in the vast and winking universe. Evil, in her own villanelle, had something to do with ex-husbands; although she never spelled it out exactly you didn't have to be a genius to pick up on it. And since southern California was owned, by and large, by ex-wives, Lorna Villanelle had become a household word almost before she knew it: Her electronic ministry made her rich and powerful before she ever even had a church, within months of the time she had first decided to be a minister.

But—you could have looked around and checked it out in our happy home—Lorna's message had little or nothing *actually* to do with us. Because we were happy. And it seemed like an ending.

Now I suppose it becomes the time to remember that in the rest of our city and our country, things weren't exactly quiet. Another war had started in Central America. The ladies in our house united in blaming men for it. But we had to go easy: Skip had lost a wife because of one global nightmare long ago, and—outside of brokering a few hundred thousand tins of quite good Argentinian beef to the leftists in some pitiable country or another—he neither profited from war nor endorsed it. And *he* was a man, the nicest we'd ever met. We began to receive increasingly crazy letters from Mrs. Chandler:

> I thank God and will thank Him always that He saw fit to vouchsafe to me the coming of the end of the (northern part of the) world, and thanks to His grace, our grandchildren, the sons of Charlene and Juanita,

our beloved daughters, may escape from the coming Holocaust. As for our beloved son Deeky (his schoolmates, as you would know very well had you seen fit to stay here with me, call him that, in a latinization of the name we gave him so long ago), he will go directly to the underground vaults of our bank and stay there. At any rate, and in any event, we have been repeatedly assured by the mayor of our own city that if there is to be a future, it belongs to prudent young men like our son. Deeky will be forever safe from military service, making, as he does, such a valuable contribution to the oligarchy. Howard, even you must realize by now that we are truly and *only* in the protecting hands of our Heavenly Father. Howard, He wants you to come home to your real family. I pray for you to come home.

Skip would never talk about these letters. Once, only once, when he saw that I had shamelessly retrieved the scraps of one of them from his wastebasket and spread them all out on our kitchen table, trying to bring order from what I considered to be madness, did he say, ''She's a good woman. She loves our children. She can't help it if she's afraid.''

She wasn't the only one. The draft in America had started up again. But by this time our poor, our wretched, our blacks and browns were not quite so compliant as they once had been. After a dozen wars in the past decade, and a dozen more in the twenty years before that, the underclasses had finally learned that there would be no reward for going away to murder women and children even poorer and sadder than they.

Instead, in the great cities, they started a war of their own. Hundreds and hundreds of draftees at induction centers, docilely took every test, and—without protest—allowed themselves to be outfitted with uniforms. They sat quietly as they were bussed away to ever more carefully guarded military bases. They diligently trained. Then they deserted, taking their guns and uniforms with them.

Let's bring the war home! the old Vietnam slogan, became the grief-stricken catch phrase of the poor. And who could blame them? They had realized, finally, from watching television, that they were as negligible as Brand X margarine, and if watching that same television had taught them the difference between good grease and bad, they learned too that there were differences between lives: Their existences were equal to the sink cleaner that couldn't remove berry stains. They were expendable, valueless. They couldn't grasp the words, but they knew the facts.

They didn't want to kill anybody, and their protests at first were symbolic. Day after sunny day, during sweet suburban noontimes, they trucked out to ''white'' high schools and junior colleges, throwing smoke bombs and squirting bullets in the air above the heads of blond ninnies who were so interested in proms and dates and grades and good universities that most of them—no matter how ''well educated''—had never even *heard* of the countries where these poor brown and black wretches had been conscripted to go, to live out the rest of their lives; give up their lives.

But parents who had so recently made the trip out West from ''nowhere'' weren't about to take a chance on sacrificing their flesh, their blood, to marauders who combined justifiable reproach with, God knows, murderous impulses, and the guns to carry them out. It was only a matter of days after these raids had begun when a group of west Los Angeles parents came to Skip (and to me), saying that there was a need for a ''new wave'' of private, middle and upper centers of education, much as there had been during the black integration scare of the early seventies. It wasn't that there weren't plenty of old-money schools, but the parents wanted places that were *safe*; unknown as well as elite. Not until Denise woke up for three days in a row with a stomachache did I realize that these three-minute segments on the nightly news really *were* more than "stories," that the war was not in some boring jungle but here, in our city.

So Oakwood flourished, and Meadow Oaks, and Oak Knoll, and Westways and West Wind, and Windward and Windhover. New schools like Golden Oaks itself sprang up all over the west side, places where, for a nominal $5,500 a year, you could save your child, unless, of course, she or he was imprudent enough to stop by Bob's Big Boy at one in the morning and get shot up like a colander by a whole other set of more serious roving urban bandits.

We decided to go with Golden Oaks, financing its loans, sending Denise there. In September of 1986 Golden Oaks was no more than four classrooms (to "handle" two hundred children from grades six through twelve), carefully hidden in a renovated warehouse in the industrial backwash of west L.A. Its student body was as distinguished as its surroundings were modest, sporting a roster of children from the homes of the city's "finest" professional people and most insecure "celebrities." Almost every lower-upper-class parent could afford Golden Oaks because it was in every case deductible. We would pay not just for our children's good time but our own. Every parent we ever met might conceivably help us in our career. Even Barbra Streisand could be "helped," and—God knows—help us.

An ad hoc consortium spent one long, frantic summer finding that building, hiring our own children to slap on coats of paint, so that disaffected Latinos might not work for us and then remember and come back with guns. We had stationery made up, and we plundered the faculties of universities: This was to be the opposite of conspicuous consumption! Many parents cherished the vagrant thought that—through the luxuries—their children might at least get a shiver of what it had been like to grow up poor.

But not really. The school's first year would begin with a combination "open house," which would treat parents to a miniature "school day," and a vast fund-raiser, with extra celebrities from movie and television land, and it was a measure of the school's financial clout that even though Denise had been accepted as a student and we'd handled their loans, I'd be attending this double event not as a regent or a trustee or even a "Founder" but as a simple parent, and damn glad of that.

So, at five o'clock one muggy September evening, I found myself, with fifty other conscientious parents, folded into a desk made for a person half my size, fighting claustrophobia in the "Einstein Room," a windowless, airless prison cell meant to protect our children from the worries of the larger world. The next two hours were filled with bells and schedules and minilectures from excellent professors who, most of them, had been denied tenure at UCLA.

The new headmaster rose in the middle of this truncated "day" to speak of donors, fellowships, and the like. Our first scholarship recipients turned out to be entirely young Korean musicians—a nationality (and occupation) that certainly had no say, either in the present war we were conducting abroad or in the one that threatened us at home. The parents whose hands had been waving earnestly in the air just moments before—clasped them noncommittally in their laps. How, after all these years, could school still be so dull?

Who was listening anyway? Who cared about any of that stuff? For here, finally, in this forbidding cement-block room, was our own "high school" raised to exquisite purity. To be old, or even a parent, no longer pertained. Who could call Jane Fonda old? Who could look at that independent producer Tony Bill and call him Dad? Or Franz deGeld, that other independent producer who was fast beating Bill at his very own game? Or Sheri North, who lived at the beach on a diet of nuts and seeds and looked younger, more beautiful by far, than she had twenty-five years before? Or Barbra herself? My classmates for those two hours were eternal children; most of them great beauties, crouched at secondhand desks and concentrating on looking good.

Then, behind me, and a little to the left, I heard a sigh, a guttural aspiration, and a whisper behind the palm of a hand, barely heard, but heartfelt: *"What shit!"* It echoed my thoughts about whatever the hell the headmaster was saying, but it raised the hair on my forearms as well. I covered my eyes as if from the sun (what a high school gesture *that*, coming back to me after twenty-something years) and, peeking back under my hand, saw, shrouded in a silk turban, hidden by reflector glasses, the collar of her white linen jacket turned up almost to her cheekbones, the now-famous Lorna Villanelle. I hadn't seen her in years. She'd been whispering, she told me later, just to get my attention, and she waved to me, when she got it, with a furtive three-finger waggle.

"And so we hope, in the coming months, to instill in this new 'family' of ours, a sense of unselfishness, of . . ."

"Bullshit!" the lips under the reflector glasses shaped in exaggerated scorn, and all the parents in their seats shifted uncomfortably. The bell finally rang, and we adjourned—in family cars and limos—for the fun part of the evening, because I truly believe all of us, even then, never gave up our faith in a good party.

That first fund-raiser, held for parents and "friends of Golden Oaks School" as well as for all the children who made up this small but diamond-studded student body, was held at the home of Sid Jacobson, who later that year would be at the center of so many Hollywood scandals. Whether he actually *stole* all that money from his own movie studio, he certainly put it to good use—the double tennis court, the pre-Columbian art protected in glassed cabinets—which some envious guests said certainly didn't show Sid's taste but only the good taste of the pre-Columbians. The estate was renowned as a showplace, and against the burly chatter of the outdoor party placed carefully on an enormous veranda that ran the length of the mansion in the style of colonial India, you saw—and heard—the whispers of big-time business.

I got there late. As I was ushered by a servant to the doors of the library, which led in turn to an atrium and thence to the noisy veranda, I hesitated, watching money being made, or so I told myself. I gazed at Franz deGeld, the independent producer, at the center of a small circle of young men, lit from above by track lights. How could I not? At that time he was good for a two-page spread in the Calendar Section; I, good for only one. Both of us had already been profiled in *California* magazine—not for our work but for our "lifestyles." I for my canyon hideaway, he for the Jacuzzi in his beachside offices. *You* knew him, what can I say about him? He affected an Austrian accent, although there were those who swore they'd known him twenty years ago at L.A. High as plain Len Bast. His hair was as gold and thick as the name he had taken, his skin porcelain-clear as a nineteenth-century doll. Eyes, deep blue, opened and shut with an almost perceptible click. Cheeks smooth and unblemished. A visage of utter, steely indifference to everything, always. Forearms always exposed, always tan. A wife, serious, beautiful and careworn, his own Dorian Gray, always at his side. A series of sweaters—you saw them in careful publicity pictures—ice grey, ice blue, ice peach, worn pushed to the elbow, and an adjunct three-quarters-of-an-inch of cuff of starched white shirt between that fine tan skin, that deep cashmere. There were those who said his brain was completely blown by coke, and those who said he was fine. Certainly there were evenings, at Michael's, or the Venture Inn, or some other très élégant beach restaurant where the reflected glare

from white walls turned his face into a death mask, but
that was probably the effect he was aiming for. Most days,
most nights, he sustained the better image, the bachelor
boy with the loyal mother-wife: his mask of contempt and
emptiness perfectly composed.

And if you ask why was I glancing at all that—well,
nobody's perfect. One man looked up and then fell silent.
I went on out past them, through the atrium, onto the
veranda.

Volcanic eruptions on the other side of the world had
given us weeks of spectacular sunsets. A wide, endless
green sea of grass washed down to a private lagoon, rem-
iniscent of the South Seas. A ragged line of absurdly tall
palms scratched black lines against the persimmon sky,
marking off the boundaries of this estate and the next,
known in the neighborhood only semisardonically as the
Kingdom of Gregory Peck.

Skip was down in Buenos Aires this week, attending to
family matters, and to business. I had come alone tonight
(or, rather, just with Denise, who had arrived in another
car), wearing close to five thousand dollars' worth of pure
silk, thick cotton, and rough-cut sapphires. Nothing's too
good where the kids are concerned! I'd been right on the
button. For a garden party where the Jacobsons had extended themselves only as far as unwashed strawberries
still in their lugs, cases of Poland Water, and unmarked
carafes of bad white wine, the guests were decked out in
tropical finery fallen angels might envy. I never could exactly think of us as living in "Hollywood," but I can
name the names and recreate the world: All the stars were
there, and those professors from UCLA, and Joan Palev-
sky, whose devotion to good causes is still remembered,
and the Aaron Spellings, who naturally had been invited
to be trustees, and Marcia Seligson from the Hunger Project, and plenty of the very best *dogs*, whippets and afghan
hounds and Belgian shepherds.

After the dogs came the ordinary parents who had paid
two hundred dollars a crack for this evening—in addition
to their tuition. Good-looking couples gamely sporting
name tags that had their kids' names in parentheses underneath. The last names were almost always different.
But it could never be said that these parents weren't conscientious. Their faces showed it, their bodies showed it.

I said hello to Barbra. I thought it was my right, since
she had an account at the bank. She remembered me without a glance at my name tag. I said hello to Jackie Joseph
of Actors and Others for Animals; I said hello to Marina
Bokelman, whom I'd known during my first marriage as a
student of folklore. It was a measure of something that she
had become by now a *professional storyteller*, a real one.
People paid to hear her tell stories; and they were terrific
ones, about slaves who outsmarted their owners, about
John the "Conqueror-Root." Marina would open that
week at the Troubador. She too was in finery: long skirts
of dirty green silk with gypsy pockets. Even with no children she had been asked to be a trustee. And within the
hour, when the Golden Oaks' parents would adjourn to the
far end of the veranda to hear a half hour of brand-new
patter from a comedian, and the children of the upper
school carried by chartered bus to watch the UCLA Bruins
in one of their first games of the season, the kids of the
middle school would gather in the library to hear Marina's
stories.

I had an inward, nascent shiver of esprit de corps.
Why, I was *proud* to be a Golden Oaks parent! And when,
again, I crossed the veranda to be with Lorna, already at
the center of a half-circle of half-suspicious, half-envious
other parents, I was tickled pink.

Lorna turned away from her group, and we stood together—our elbows braced on an ornate balustrade—and
looked out across the grounds. In our smiles, our steady
grins, was the iron of triumph. The grass that slanted away

from us here on this deep and luxurious evening was so different from the raw green threads of that so-distant university where we had started, blotted out now by asphalt and sullen hordes of dull Chicanos. But Lorna said nothing beyond, "Are you sending Denise here? Letty will have someone to play with. I suppose they're too old to play now, but whatever it is they do . . . spend the night at each other's houses. . . ."

The past! The future! It seems to me now I talk about the *present*, those events that seem so recent they surely *must* qualify as present, and yet, at that time, the school had not started, had not even convened one real class, except that truncated "day" for besotted parents. There had not been, as yet, one student party, not one of those disasters that prompted disgruntled parents in that first (and only) year to say that the Golden Oaks coat of arms should be a totaled Mercedes rampant on a floss silk tree . . . garlanded by mourning parents, all divorced.

We glanced, together, out across the wide, velvet green softness where six grades of children, objects of this extraordinary endeavor, ran and played. As the couples behind us exchanged glances, Lorna and I could see and feel—and I know I loved it, wanted it—the *attention*; we reveled in it, in a quiet way, of course. We were the evangelist and the banker, and had been friends half our lives! Arm in arm, we watched the children play.

There would have been Philip McCan, son of the actor with the beautifully stitched harelip, and Farley Johnson, who—later that year—so taunted his father about the sexual charms of his new and nubile stepmom that the father blammed the son, removing all his front teeth in one blow. The son's revenge? Phoning the *Enquirer* and arranging for a front-page photo. I remember a nice kid, Mary Ellen Reid, standing alone and crying, and Franz deGeld's little girl (one of his two children), perfect in grey walking shorts and enormous hornrimmed glasses. And, of course,

Lorna's Letty and my Denise—enjoying one of the last rare times before they'd have to straighten up and be ladylike—running and rolling and shouting.

My eyes weren't what they had been, and it took me two or three minutes to see that it was a pick-up soccer game they were murdering each other with, Letty winning, playing with my tough little Denise who had the game in her Australian blood, making points, making the guys look like rag dolls; but when you thought about that, it was easy to do . . . the ninth-grade boys, compared to their robust female companions, were scrabbly, shrill, weak, worried.

Some girls watched and most boys played. Letty and Denise stayed right in there shouting, pushing. Most kids played as if they'd never seen a ball before but with a kind of overriding rage (or were all youngsters like that?). Occasionally the adults would call down from the terrace, "Peter, *watch* it, will you?" Or, "Rachel, stay out of the way, dear . . . ," but for the most part their glances were perfunctory; their conversation stayed within safe boundaries: a garden party on the veranda.

Lorna and I spoke in half-whispers.

"So? How's it going?"

"The good doctor, Isadore? Dr. Israel? He's getting alimony payments from *me* now."

"You're *kidding*!"

"Listen, I'm lucky. He says I not only took the best years of his life, but I stole all his material."

I could think of nothing to say.

"You know, now that I'm rich, I'm reading the business pages. I see your name all the time . . ."

"God knows, I see you."

It was taking forever to get dark, but night was inexorably catching up with us. Down on the lawn, the game was getting out of hand. From the sidelines, where she'd been watching with the other girls, a tiny Korean cellist, imported by the trustees for her matchless musical talent, suddenly roused herself and ran, with *kim chee* shrieks, into the center of the game. A fat kid with a blubber butt and huge spectacles tied by leather thongs about his head ran her down, jumped right on her, leaving her writhing on the grass. Lorna and I both moved—she stepping forward and I back—to look for oriental parents, if I could find any—when I felt Lorna's hand steely on my arm.

"Shit," she whispered.

The fat boy had knocked down someone else, a skinny child with wild hair and pale legs that flashed as he skidded over on his side, just in time to get the brunt of an avenging Korean brother as he ran screeching after Fats and came down with an audible *crunch* on the skinny kid's arm. The terrible lost howl of a child in pain echoed across the lawn; past all the elms, the maples, the birds-of-paradise in banks, and far into the darkened Kingdom of Gregory Peck. The parents who'd heard, froze, like kids themselves in a game of statues.

The little boy lay splayed and motionless by now. His cries had stopped and his one good arm worked wildly in its socket; he was getting ready to lose consciousness. His left arm lay flat upon the lawn, bent not at the elbow but two inches above it. A good inch of blue-white bone protruded, like a broken celery stalk, out of bluish skin and torn pink flesh, by now just barely visible in the violet light. Lorna followed me as I ran down. I could *feel* her behind me, that familiar prickly wall of energy. When we got to the kid, I stepped back, or rocked back on my heels, to let her do something and saw her hesitating. *"You mean you aren't* . . . *?"* I heard myself say the words.

Then, through the growing crowd of horrified parents, we heard heavy steps. The father bent over the son, fell to his knees and looked up, looked around—for justice, for divine intervention. It was Franz deGeld, with his perfect tan—white shirt, cashmere, face, chinos, shoes, socks,

his glinting hair of gold. His indifference had been
wrenched from him. Even in the dusk you could see the
pulse at his throat. That face was famous, more than famous; and it showed now a genuine anguish most of his
colleagues would have given six points of any film's gross
profit to see.

You could almost *hear* the brains of the Hollywood
wives who peered excitedly from the balcony—staying on
that hard surface so as not to ruin their shoes in grass and
mud. They were *on the scene*, for once; not third-, not
fourth- or fifth-hand behind the dreaded childhood cancer,
the unexpected leukemia, the sudden teenage death from
drugs or suicide, or the simple car smash-up against the
tree.

The wives were what I noticed then, for those seconds.
I sneered at their helplessness, as usual; their inability to
be anything more than ornaments, ever.

In that minute, two minutes, an eternity of time digited
away. The boy by now had fainted. Franz deGeld, kneel-
ing, appeared to be afraid to move his son. His beautiful
eyes reproachfully scanned the gathering crowd, who
didn't or couldn't speak. The kids had run away. The Korean girl got up, grimly, cradling her arm, and came over
to watch.

Lorna lingered, still and grave, at a safe distance from
the now-unconscious boy, until his exquisite father looked
straight at her. She'd said on television often enough to
expect a miracle, and perhaps he was a secret watcher.

She reached up and pulled off her turban, dropped it to
the ground, folded her dark glasses, and handed them to
me. She took off her white linen Jacket and stood shim-
mering in purple silk, her hair a wild cloud of red-gold.
Then I saw her fold down into him, crumple her body like
a night bird alighting, down into the muddy grass. She
fastened her head into the crook of Franz deGeld's neck.
The two knelt silently with the boy between them. All

across the estate, safe wives shut their eyes. There were some things they didn't want to see, devoted their lives to not seeing.

Time stopped again, and by the time Callie deGeld came trotting down the grassy escarpment, her hair messed, her face tear-stained, her dainty sandals broken and flopping off her feet, she was there only for the breaking away. Lorna rocked back on her heels, her face chalky white in the gathering darkness, her eyes lidded.

"Your son has had a bad fall," she said—and I got an idea, for an instant, of what a *drag* it must have been to have Christ around at parties. "You might want to take him to an emergency room for a check-up."

Even as she spoke, the father had gathered the boy in his arms, rocked back himself, and stood, staggering slightly from his burden. *You don't want to do that*! I almost said, or heard my mind saying, but Lorna commanded me silent with a look, and I saw, in the dark, the kid sleeping now, his mended arm hooked up and around his father's neck. The wife sniffed, looked, wiped her nose on her silk sleeve, and trudged after him, up and out of sight and into the Mercedes that the valets—hired boys from UCLA—had the sense to have waiting.

What else can I say about that night? For a year they called it the night little Matthew deGeld took that awful fall. It was also the beginning of Lorna's affair with Franz, which made no difference to speak of in Callie's life; it wasn't exactly a new deal for her. And it marked the official beginning of Golden Oaks School, which came up, after that remarkable evening, with something like a half-million endowment. Every grown-up there ended up kicking in $1,500. Joan Palevsky kicked in a hundred thou; so did the Jacobsons, and so did Franz himself.

I suppose selfishly I'd have to say that marked my first real entrée into the highest level of southern California society. I'd banked on that, of course, quite literally—figuring that my investment in Denise would be one for my career, but I hadn't thought to see the dividends so early. Lorna spoke to Franz, who spoke to the Golden Oaks headmaster, and I, still with no real husband and only a token job in the world of real finance, was put on the Board of Trustees and for only the fourth time had the absolutely exhilarating pleasure of seeing my own name halfway down the left margin of some very very heavy stationery.

It was a night of beginnings, that party. Many people spoke of and thought of it in the year to come. Lorna and I were friends again, acting out our same relentless—some would say pointless—friendship, and right from scratch: "He called me! I *knew* he'd call me! But . . . so . . . what do you think I should do?" And that voice was not always Lorna's on the phone, but sometimes mine this time— although she may have said the same words on the phone the following day or later that same afternoon.

Because as Franz and Callie had taken little Matt off to the UCLA emergency room, and whispering couples had begun to decide that in fact they hadn't seen what they'd seen, I felt another prickle of energy. I took it to be some last fallout from what Lorna had done, but then looked down to see an arm—as if it were my very own arm!— offering me a glass of champagne. Do you understand? Someone had come to stand behind me, his face by my hair, his breath lightly on my neck, his chest to my shoulder blades, but lightly, lightly. My own arms hung helpless at my sides; I still held Lorna's dark glasses, but it was as if my own arm swung up with that champagne. I waited for it, I really did, for it to ascend to my lips, and when it didn't, reached for it with my left hand and swung around to see part of myself, as if in an old, cracked mirror.

Everything I'd ever studied to get rid of was there, in front of me. The weight I'd dieted off was there, on him.

The round cheeks I knew to be my own were there, on
him. The silly grin I had to keep sternly off my face during
business meetings was there, plastered across his not-ter-
ribly bright, very good-natured face. He'd been drinking,
he swayed slightly. His head bent in at me at a peculiarly
intense angle. *"Shiker,"* I heard some Jewish professional
behind him say disdainfully, or—no—just objectively.

"Do you have children attending here?" I could hear
the schoolmarm voice of the lady with the (precious) stones
in her briefcase, the landowner, the parent.

He peered at me quizzically. Was he seeing what I saw?
All the things he might have seen? A responsible, acquis-
itive person, who, even when she learned a little magic,
used it to get something to improve her situation—a house,
a car, a grade, a position, a little *respect*, for Christ's
sake? This chubby man wore a loud plaid suit and an ascot
tie; it was a good bet that no one had respected *him* since
his mother had taken her first look and said, *"Oy vey!"*
or, "The saints preserve us," or, *"Why me?"*

But he didn't seem to care.

"No," he said, and gave a foolish grin.

"No, what?"

"No, I'm not a parent. They needed some extras to
dress the house, and here I am. Don't you need to fill that
glass up? Don't you want to fill that up?"

His name was Hal. He was Armenian or Ukrainian,
forgive me if I can't remember what he was now. His
parents had been done away with in an old-country mas-
sacre. He had a million girlfriends, including a million-
airess who was always getting married again when her
husbands' fortunes dwindled. He took a gold chain out of
his pocket and gave it to me, folded it into my hand with
Lorna's glasses.

"Don't lose this," Hal said to me. "My grandmother
gave it to my father just before she died. I think you ought
to have it." I found out later that he carried those chains

by the gross in his car, and that, yes, they were real gold. He'd never done a day's work in his life; he said he was too busy. "I can't even get around to getting the newspapers out of the back seat of my car! I can't even get my taxes straightened out! I can't even keep the rents up on my building!" For he owned a false-Tudor-building business in the Valley.

We drank about fourteen more champagnes; he'd made sure to find where the real stock was—upstairs in Mrs. Jacobson's own sitting room, in a small refrigerator next to the chaise longue—and we reclined, or he did, on that elegant piece of period furniture, while I sat on a Louis XVI chair and listened to bits and pieces of his nonexistent career, which he spoke of with ardor and perfect belief. But his real interest was food, as his round figure confirmed.

"I *know* you eat at Michael's, but do you eat at Scratch? Do you know that when that woman who owns it had a miscarriage she was back in the next day in a nightgown and overcoat to see what they were . . ."

"Her husband," I interrupted eagerly, "has invented a, what do you call it, a French fry dispenser . . ."

"And a foot mobile. No, a mobile *foot!*"

In the very old days, there was a word you never hear now, a doppelganger, a human, man or woman, who walks and talks and thinks like you. Hal, Prince Hal, I came to call him, was that for me. And though *I* had the job, it was his generosity, his refusal to care about anything at all, that I came to count upon, and as the days ahead grew—darker—I want you to believe that I hardly noticed. But why do I lie to you, especially now? Of course I noticed.

Waking with a start at five in the morning, even earlier, reaching over for Skip to find myself alone, I'd get up, and after resentfully going to the bathroom, feel my way down the stairs because the sun wasn't up yet. I'd go into Skip's own room without knocking, and he'd be hunched over his tickertape, in the dark; his bathrobe drawn tight around him. His face, when he looked at me, grey.

"What *is* it?" I'd demand, irritably, not wanting to know at all, middle-aged lady nagging an elderly man, and he'd twist his face into a smile. "It can only help us," he'd say. "Our investments are safe, and you only have daughters. And Deeky is safe." But the sadness on the face of that good man would break your heart—if you had a heart. So I protected myself the way we all protected ourselves in those very first months. We watched the news, and hardened our hearts, and I . . . I hardly thought about it. I only thought about what I should wear to work, and what I'd say to Lorna when she called. I just kept going out to lunch. I gained twenty pounds again, from champagne alone, and became a regular at Charmer's Market, because where else would a charmer eat lunch?

I learned to not listen about Felicia, the famed heiress Hal said he loved, the way I'd learned to discount the news. They're *always* saying those things, aren't they? What counts is now, *now*, this fruit, this wine, this smiling face, this sappy joke. That is to say, nothing counts now, at all.

Denise came home from school every day with her good clothes stained and in tatters from strenuous pick-up games, reciting new phrases in Latin and even Greek, delivering wonderful adolescent tirades about the social injustice of rich kids like her getting to go to good schools while the poor were ordered to go south to kill people. Golden Oaks was touchingly straight up, in its short life, about telling the truth.

But there was the new stuff, the real stuff, that Denise didn't talk about, because they didn't teach it over at Golden Oaks. Our board had made the decision to downplay the war. To show that even governments could be merciful, the really terrifying dispatches were saved for the very last time slots on the eleven o'clock news. It was interesting to think that all across America other boards and clubs and investors and people everywhere were making the decision without talking much about it. Don't scare the kids.

Because one reason that an absolutely authentic miracle in the home of one of Hollywood's richest and most corrupt moguls didn't get any media coverage, ever, even when there were "people" there from four separate independent stations, was that at the same time Franz and Callie called for their limo, and Lorna put little Lim Jin Twan back in tip-top cello-playing order, a skinny woman from Channel 9 heard a beep from the electronic device concealed in her designer jeans, and the Channel 9 van skidded up behind the deGeld car to take her back to the station, pronto. Some one of those low-life, unevolved Central American patrols had finally used some small—oh, I hate to say the *word* now—the hated adjective that modifies "device." The device lay in a small damp crevasse of some third-rate jungle, and by its invisible smoke, its lively death rays, killed everyone and everything around and about. Who had done it? No one knew. You couldn't get close enough to find out the name on the weapon's casing. And it was small, that first time, very small, fewer than 5,000 killed. And every side was temperate. No one wanted to "overreact." And the whole story might have been a lie, like that "yellow rain" everyone had talked about a decade before, and then someone on National Public Radio went to the trouble to find out that it was either bee pollen or bee shit, I don't remember.

So the lady on Channel 9 made sure to say it might be a mistake, or misreportage, or at least the victims had stayed in the four-figure range, and besides it was far away, as in every other jungle war we'd ever fought. Until (some nights, at one in the morning) you'd see a close-up of a child on television, his flesh charred yellow like a broiled fish, gasping for air, his face turning from side to side, and you'd know, well, yes, for an instant you'd know. But what was the point of *knowing*? Even now I thank God or the universe for my own last weeks of thoughtless laughter, for Felicia's borrowed finery, the magnums of finest champagne, the obdurate refusal of *one* person, I knew, at least—Prince Hal—to think of anything but giggling.

One night I came home, woozy, having put away a bottle or two at lunch and having spent the afternoon with my new buddy Hal at Scratch, or Michael's, acting silly: There can't be anything wrong, can there be anything *wrong*, I'd ask myself, with just a few *laughs*, you know?

When I came home I saw Denise in the kitchen, in an apron, heating up frozen hors d'oeuvres.

"What's . . . ?"

She jerked her head upwards, and I thanked her silently in my heart for not asking, as she might well have, for not screeching, *Where the fuck have you been?*

"Aurora's come home . . ."

And as I began to say, querulously, defensively, "So? Since she's been a courier, doesn't she come home every ten days and stay three days and leave the next? . . . Not that I'm not glad to see her, of course," my younger went on, worried, "Skip's son has come with her. They're in the living room."

I went upstairs, blinking against a wave of drunkenness, and stood in the door, swaying. My older daughter looked at me in one frozen moment of disapproval before she got up and came across the room to kiss my cheek. But (I like to believe) my public persona prevailed, and as the two men, young and old, stood, formally, in their dark suits, I regained enough possession of myself to kiss Skip—lightly, lightly—and to shake hands in the Latin manner with Deeky. I even asked after his mother, recalling that since our winter was their summer, and since I knew she was always troubled by the heat, I hoped the season was treating her kindly. I even (in my memory, at least) extended an invitation on behalf of my country, if not myself, for Estelle to spend a few weeks up here in the States.

The atmosphere in our usually peaceful living room was . . . how can I find words to describe it?

"My mother sends her best wishes to you, Mrs. Langley," said Deeky Chandler, who had left his home twenty-six years earlier as a cute four-year-old named Dick, "but she has asked me to convey this message. My mother has sent me to tell you that you have had the consolations of my father's company long enough. It is time for you to do what is right, to return him to his rightful family."

Aurora looked down at her manicure. It occurred to me that in her many trips down there this year she must have met Skip's wife, even befriended her.

"It is not our whim, or even God's whim," Deeky went on. "It is God's law. I'm sure you have heard, what God has . . ."

"Well that's the lamest shit I ever heard in *my* life!" It was Denise, her face flushed from the oven, and from indignation. "If your mother is so crazy about Skip, why doesn't she just come up *here*? This is America, isn't it? It's a free world!"

Aurora looked at me with incredible sadness.

"Deeky," Skip said, "I can't go back. I know that what we all fear may happen. It . . . will happen. But I can't go along with it. I wish you'd . . . I want you to tell your mother that, that it's not a question of 'love.' It's principle. I'd be a coward in my eyes if I were to go back. Listen to those words, '*to go back!*' I . . ."

Aurora stood up. "Mother. Denny. Deeky has asked me to go back with him, and I will. I want you to know he has asked me to be his wife. I have already converted to Catholicism. I believe . . ." and here she looked at me with both anger and love, "that all of us up here have done something wrong. That the church must be right when it says that there is an original sin. I believe that what I should do is return with Deeky. We, all of us, should submit ourselves to a larger will, because . . ."

"Afraid you're going to fry?" My younger daughter spoke in a storm of tears; she threw her tray of hors d'oeuvres on the floor.

"Denise! Come with us! It's not too late. And it's not a joke. The end of the world *is* . . ."

But Skip said, "Let's talk about this sensibly. I'm absolutely delighted that you and Aurora have come to this agreement. May I suggest that the little house where Estelle and I used to live, above the banks of La Plata, would be a perfect place for the two of you to spend your first years? Aurora, I couldn't be more pleased. For many years now I've thought of you as a daughter. For that to finally come to pass is a great blessing. Deeky, please convey my very best to your mother. . . ."

"You're not coming home?" Deeky's voice quavered.

Skip spoke directly to me. "I don't stay for such a simple thing as love. Please forgive me, dearest, because we'll be friends and partners forever. It's that I've found my place. Barbarians will not move me from it."

"So," Denise said, sniffing. "Can I be maid of honor?"

Aurora took her sister's hand. "Can you come with us tonight?"

"Tonight?" Denise flinched, and came over to stand by me.

And I understood in that minute, in a cold shudder of death itself, that Aurora was lost to me forever. Beyond that, I saw (what I imagined to be) her vision: a burnt world and, at its bottom, a few strict pilgrims, living in purgatory until they died, hoping for a dubious reward.

"Oh, honey!" I cried. "Is it right? Are you sure? Is this what you must do?"

She wept then. "I'm so afraid. I know it's going to

happen. This is the only thing *to* do.'' And they would
talk to us no longer. They left within minutes.

The next day I woke at five. It was a beautiful morning.
The sky was eggshell blue and hummingbirds flung themselves against the plate-glass windows. As always in those
last weeks, Skip was already out of bed. I went down to
his room, where, the drapes still drawn, he bent in his
bathrobe over the tickertape.

''Another weapon,'' he said, ''this time in southern
Mexico. I imagine this is what they were talking about last
night. Twenty thousand killed.''

''They're gone,'' I said. ''Do you think I'll ever see
Aurora again?''

Skip looked at me and shrugged, almost jauntily. ''We
can go anywhere, Edie. We can even go down there. I
don't care, as long as I'm with you. But . . . I don't know.
I think it's wrong to . . . I don't think . . . I believe if you
allow them to frighten you, they've won their game before
they've started it.''

''Nothing's going to happen! Not a goddamn thing! It's
crazy! It's melodramatic! It's stupid! It's nuts! Imagine
those kids going off in the night like that! Making those
melodramatic goodbyes. I think it's a lot of crap, is what
I think.''

Skip watched another three or four lines of information
click its way out of the machine before he spoke. ''I didn't
get much sleep last night,'' he said. ''Suppose we both
take the day off and go to the beach. Maybe go to Michael's for lunch, and then . . . I don't know, drive up the
coast, spend the night. Unless you're busy?''

I knew what he was saying, what he was asking. ''Hell,
no,'' I said. ''I'm ready! And what you did last night for
me, staying here, I'll never forget it.''

''When I said it wasn't love,'' Skip muttered, pulling
the drapes, opening the gloomy little den-bedroom to a

mad panorama of green trees and yellow acacia and delirious hummingbirds, "I want you to know I wasn't entirely telling the truth."

PART 2

And the earth threw them up one after the other. . . . And suddenly they stirred and swayed and rose up in the same orderly rows: the earth was throwing up new bodies, and they were lifting the first ones upward. . . .

—Leonid Andreyev
The Red Laugh

WAITING AROUND

JUNE 1987

"HAVEN'T YOU, I MEAN, HAVEN'T YOU EVER BEEN WAKED up by the *bailiff*? I mean, you're lying there sound asleep, you think you've got a moment's peace, trying to log a little shuteye, and all of a sudden it sounds like the world is coming to an end, the *house* is coming to an end, bells are ringing, someone's screaming, and Felicia's pinching your neck, *don't answer it, don't answer it! They don't know we're here!* So you pull your blanket up around your poor chubby shoulders and put the pillow up over your head, and come to find out six months ago she's bought four Hakada Japanese dolls worth fifteen hundred dollars apiece and hidden them in the closet so you won't find out about them and *get upset,* because you can't pay for them, because you're working for the Pasadena post office for eight hundred and fifty a month . . ."

His face lit up with a soft, sweet, secret smile. The setting sun put a pink light around him and on him. He made a wide, soft gesture with his left hand, palm up, moving out and down, from north to south. "But this is pretty nice, now, you see."

Far in front of us the turquoise glitz of the Pacific. Between us and it, palm trees; then that living strip of bright green grass along the cliffs of Santa Monica Beach, against a thoroughfare where even the traffic was a pleasure to get caught in, made up, as it was, of tan Mercedes and silver Porsches, and even the Volkses were shiny lemon yellow. The air was sparkling clean and sixty-seven degrees. Across Ocean Avenue, on that narrow, grassy picnic ground that stretched as far as our eyes could see, old ladies walked sedately two by two, a few college men roller-skated considerately, and families got out of station wagons carrying wicker baskets, sacks of briquets, folding tables, and checkered cloths. What few children there were here were not boisterous.

"How does she keep her plants watered?" I hated Hal's bi-coastal girlfriend, the more so because I was the recipient of her generosity. Though I knew these things shouldn't matter, I was still shocked at the idea, yes, the *idea*, that when Felicia lost a button on a Galanos dress, she went out to buy another dress and not another button.

"What I can't figure out is why—no offense—she goes on seeing you."

His wide, sweet face eclipsed. "She needs a friend. *He* can't understand that. She needs a friend, that's all. But she needed *him*, because I couldn't support her."

"But . . ."

"Have you eaten anywhere good lately?"

"I want to know why she goes on seeing you."

"She's not *seeing* me. She doesn't *see* me."

The sun fell into the ocean and the whole world turned a deep blue-grey. Lonely little fires twinkled along the strand.

Out on Felicia's balcony we ate artichoke hearts run under the broiler with feta cheese and a single walnut half. Schramsberg champagne. President Nixon had taken it to China with him. In 1975 I had met the maître d' of the Tour d'Argent one afternoon on vacation in Barcelona, and he said Nixon knew how to eat. I missed that guy!

We were going to move on to endive brushed with strong

olive oil and run under that same broiler, then fresh raspberries and more champagne. It was summer, and the evening refused to cool. I put my feet up on the balcony's
edge, tilted my head back and looked at the stars. Down
on the strand, Frusen Glädjé had a cart that sold ice cream
cones with a sign that said, "Open till the very end!" I
wished I had one, but I wouldn't get it tonight.

In a while I'd call home to say I'd be "a little late."
Geez! I'm only talking about ten days, *at the most*, that I
didn't go home, in those last three weeks.

"Hal? Can you tell me how she keeps those plants
watered? Isn't she in *Cairo* now?" I'm not sure he heard
me in the kitchen, but I knew the answer. It must have
been one of those plant services; they brought in the plants
and hung them up, and they were still coming in to water
them, conscientious till the very end.

Hal came back with espresso and a sectioned orange
drenched in rakia. "Wow!" I said. Because the fumes
went through my nose into my soul. I'd been in the sun
all day and my skin was already on fire.

He put a big square hand on my shoulder.

"Listen! No problem!" My voice squeaked a little. He
didn't say anything. We played with our oranges, swishing
them in our glasses. Music floated up from the strand below. A big moon came.

We'd been staying down in Felicia's apartment off and
on for about ten days. We'd been drinking and lying in the
sun, and waiting.

Actually, the waiting was fine.

HOW SCARED WE GOT!

SEPTEMBER 1986—JULY 1987

ABOUT THIS TIME MANY OF US BEGAN TO GET SCARED shitless about everything.

A Brentwood wife in one of my seminars refused to paint her swimming pool black, even though she "loved the look," because she thought her husband's enemies would somehow smuggle a shark past the house and into the yard, and then into the pool. She had four children, two in college now. Which child did she see, sliced in the water, in her mind's eye, shredded in bits, in seconds, as the shark thrashed back and forth in the limited domestic space? Or did she see her husband, or herself?

That same woman bent to look under her car every time she came back to it in a parking lot, any parking lot. What madness, what egotism! Why should anyone lie—even in this climate of domestic unrest—in the blistering Los Angeles heat, for minutes or hours, to grab the ankle of a middle-aged woman, no matter how well cared for and how prosperous? And how would that grip, no matter how steely, translate into the next few gestures, the scrambling out from under the car, still holding on to that good wife (transfixed with fear, paralyzed, unable or unwilling to kick free)? For that matter, how might that theoretical shark, thirty-five-hundred pounds of him, get carried past her tall, iron, laser-security gate, how carried past the electric alarms of the house and *around* the house, how carried out into the yard, and lifted over a second iron fence around the pool?

And yet, it's true that even from our own Golden Oaks campus, a girl went out that fateful evening with a friend to get a Bob's Big Boy hamburger—and keep in mind that Bob's hamburgers came before fast foods. In our eyes it was a ''real'' restaurant, and certainly safe.

But . . . the Golden Oaks girl and her boyfriend and a dozen other terrified after-midnight customers were ushered by thugs into a meat locker. The men (black boys, in black ski masks) opened fire, and the boyfriend died. And we read later in magazines that the girl still had trouble going into certain bathrooms because of the bright white enamel of that Big Boy charnel house, and the terror.

Most women I knew feared fire more than murder. They refused the newly fashionable wrought-iron bars for windows, for fear of being trapped inside. What was it they saw?

The fear, the first one *I* thought of, was always the fear of divorce; the sitting out on a backporch crying audibly, the lying awake in the night listening to the man you don't love breathing, the knowledge that your husband has other women and you care, or you don't care, or both. The fear, above all, that you can't figure out what's next. Remember, in this story, I was a woman who had been married (and divorced) twice. My first marriage, remember, was hardworking and pure. Posters on the wall, those theme dinners. Does the question of love even *come up* in that context?

Illusion! I say, for many women that marriage is *illusion*, as hard to pin down as the shark in the swimming pool: It's a feeling, scenery. But the fear of being left is real enough. And men know it. And so, poor things, they threaten and look out the window, and when they do leave, they're just as apt to come back—if you find another man before they find another girl—blow your head off, and throw the kids in too.

My first husband did none of that. He was gentle and decent and never paid attention to anything at all until *I* left. The day I left I cooked up a huge pot of spaghetti and left it in the refrigerator. I came back from Reno after the divorce, and the spaghetti remained, with perhaps an inch and a half of mold in fine green threads all over it. Had I really expected him to *eat* it?

My second husband slapped me around a few times before he left and never missed a chance to do me a bad turn in the ten or fifteen years after our divorce. And yet . . . the fear of his leaving was greater by far than my fear of the first failure. I'd look at his grinning face and see nothing but evil. Whether it was there or not, I've no idea. Oh, what *shit*! Of course it was there, and of course I saw it. It isn't fiction to say he did his very best to destroy me, with his fists, with his voice, with his "love" even; driving me distracted, saying it was me he really loved, even as he screwed himself silly with everyone, everyone, ev-er-y-o-oo-one, as Van Morrison says.

And what was *I* doing? Well, I don't care to discuss that, but I knew my fear of divorce was blinding, terrifying, paralyzing, etc. And looking at the kindest of men, the gentle Skip, even though we weren't even *married*, I began to think of our divorce.

Fear of being chosen last, fear of tennis, dancing, of flying—although I danced and flew incessantly, and certainly I'd arranged things so that I'd never be chosen last again. (Lion Boyce had reminded us that we create our own reality.) Cancer, of course, but listen! I have two feelings about that. Naturally, I knew by then that "cancer can be cured." But ah, then there's *cancer*, the real kind. My dad had that. To see my father, strapped alone in a hospital wheelchair under fluorescent lights, quaking in terror, convinced that representatives from Chinese tongs were lurking in the bathroom; and even after I explained to him that no, the bathroom was empty, he darted a quick and furtive look as I wheeled him past—to see him as I last saw him, and all he could say to me was, "I'm sick, I'm so sick, Edie!" And all I could say was, "I know, Dad!" And yet he'd made it so tough for his goodhearted wife, infinitely sweet son, exasperated middle-aged daughter, that of course he ended up doing time in a nursing home, and died alone. *That* was cancer!

Staring into space in a nursing home, missing your mouth with a spoonful of red Jell-O, and somewhere within you the knowledge that you've done it yourself; sulked once too often, been mean once too often, said something awful once too often, smoked too much, drunk too much, left too much fat in your diet, dropped people for no reason except you got bored with them, interrupted the conversation too many times. I could go on, but I won't.

My own greatest fear, after divorce, was the fear of going back to what I had been. That was the second thing that made me crazy. *What goes up must come down!* The ominous warning of the underclasses.

It's true I was born in poverty, in Los Angeles, and made a big deal out of it. (Then I learned that there was a Dickens character in one of his more obscure novels who also made a big deal about it, until the last chapter when his mother appeared from the distant past and said, "Well, we weren't *that* poor! He always had clean clothes and there was always food on the table!" And there went the poor guy's talk about sleeping in a ditch and never even getting to *see* a table until he was thirty-three.)

However. There was such a thing as poverty, I'll stick to that story; California poverty. L.A. in the forties. It had to do with one stunted fig tree in a postage-stamp backyard, and devil grass growing up six inches around the stucco (or peeling frame) garage. It had to do with chenille bedspreads, washed and washed until those pitiable little knots just keeled over on their side and died. It had to do with collecting the glasses that held processed cheese, and those *were* your glasses. . . .

The real poverty, the nowhere, came from waking up in the fog in the back bedroom of a two-bedroom bungalow with no trees around it. You woke up with a knot, a feeling of nausea and dread, and the look of the torn paper shade across the window was inexplicable. Somebody sometime had painted the flaking walls blue, and you didn't even know blue is associated with "blue." And after, in twenty, thirty, forty years, you still might see a flapping window shade and a twinge of the soul alerts you: *Aahh*, God. That's it, all right.

What was there to be afraid of in a painted breakfast nook with a harsh overhead light and my father with a desperate look: "There were some days, over there in Phoenix, I made a C note a week?" But nobody was listening, and there was halibut for dinner.

SUDDENLY, AFTER YEARS, AROUND THE CHRISTMAS OF 1986, I began to grieve about my lost—my *long* lost— cousin. Never pretty, never rich, brash and ungainly, badgered by her family, told she was plain to her face ("Oh—did I hurt your feelings?"), she used to sit wedged between relatives whose main sport it was to belt down half a quart of cheap brown booze and pick on the weakest like a pack of wild dogs. My cousin years before had crouched against the straightback, badly painted benches of our old breakfast nook and cried. Her only revenge would be to marry someone they hated. But her husband was a mean man. He bought a garage and made her work in it. Then he went to jail and made her live in a furnished room. Then, when he got out, he went to work selling insurance and made her be a typist. And he kept his hat on in the house at all times.

At first my cousin was happy. She had her children, her husband drove her mother nuts. What more could any woman (in our knowledge, at that time) want?

My first memory of her marriage, any marriage. Another two-bedroom house to the south of the city: we'll say Inglewood, or the City of Industry. An unmown lawn and a sheet tacked up across the living room window. A sea of crud—newspapers, cigarette butts, coffee cups—across the floor of every tiny room (she was one bad housekeeper), except for the back bedroom, where the space had been made tidy for the kids' return from their paternal grandma. The blankets had been pulled up across thin pillows; toys, broken and bent, stacked up across the bureau, the floor swept clean, and on the bed a card, carefully printed, WELCOME HOME. When I saw it, as an adolescent, a heartbreaking surge of grief swept over me. No one had ever written such a card for me, nor ever would. My cousin looked at me in pride. (How old could she have been then? No more than twenty-five.) See? She silently pointed out. It is possible to civilize oneself, to live within certain restrictions, not always to go for the throat.

Ten years later it even seemed that she had lucked into our dream in the West—sun and fun, love and family affection. That guy she'd married did love her and he worked hard. It was his dream that he should be able to give her "everything." Poor dude! By that time he had bought her a "lovely home"—four bedrooms, a hair's breadth from a street full of other houses just like it. It was his dream that she should have a swimming pool, and he found contractors to dig it: They, in an excess of enthusiasm, began digging where the back porch ended, and kept on digging right to the fence. He turned this into a virtue, explaining that after breakfast you could take a dip simply by leaving the kitchen and not paying attention.

The last time I saw Teresa was the Christmas she was thirty-five. I was between marriages, alone, with one daughter. Each year she invited all her family, so that close to midnight, after the turkey, a mean-tempered poker game, and plenty of bourbon, her husband might noisily pitch us all out again. Their garage, this year, had been turned into a "playroom." There was a pool table in there, and an older son cued the ball around with sullen companions. A daughter whispered ostentatiously into the phone. The whole place had been recently carpeted in lemon-yellow shag, and at my cousin-in-law's order, each of us sat with a coffee cup full of detergent on the rug beside us, so that if we spilled something, we could clean it up immediately.

And my cousin lounged in that smoke-filled, tiny living room laughing, her Christmas present, a full-length mink coat, across her shoulders, although it was a sunny California day of about seventy degrees. She must have been on her forty-seventh drink, and—how can I say what I feel here?—I knew that the ritual throwing-out of her side of the family would come earlier this year, and I couldn't blame her for the carpet or the coat or her husband. I'd like to say I rose with dignity from my place on the Naugahyde couch and said goodbye to them forever, but I stayed for dinner and left only a half hour or so before the guy with the hat got dangerous.

And, so, talking of fear, while some people feared singing in public or being crushed by a fire engine on its way to a fire, or the marauding blacks, or "failure," I had two fears. Divorce, like I said. And I feared *them*—what I had come from—and their life. When they'd curled their hair, I'd worn mine straight; while they'd droned on about insurance, I'd pursued the arts. Since I thought them so all-fired *stupid*, I strove for knowledge, and never in any of my houses would you ever have been able to find a liquor tinted brown. But then that spring I got *scared*. What if something happened, a Depression, or I had a stroke? What if —like my cousin—I went back to what I *had* been?

In fact, let's get serious, I was frightened to death of everything. Afraid of steam rollers and derailed trains; chemical spills, landslides, brushfires, floods; and being the last one chosen on the team. Afraid of the blind, afraid of the deaf. Afraid my children would die. Afraid of . . . who would fix my television antenna; how would I find the courthouse?

SOMETIME IN THE LATE SEVENTIES, AFTER MY FATHER'S disease had been diagnosed, I drove with the kids down the coast to San Diego and across the border into Tijuana. My daughters and I picked our way through hordes of Mexicans (who some people we knew were afraid of) and evidence of heavy poverty (which some people we knew were afraid of) and made our way past bumpy roads to the Contreras clinic (which some people we knew were certainly afraid of).

A small hotel, and a man watching a small black and white TV. No, the medical staff wasn't around today. But we might want to look in the "health restaurant" across the street. We trailed down a dirt road to a storefront, which in addition to *antojitos* and *rico menudo* offered *jugo de naranjas* and yoghurt. It was closed tight shut. I felt terrible about returning home with no information on a possible miracle cure for my dad. We walked back to the clinic, past the crumbling hotel, to several miniature quonset huts. Bending over to look in through the single windows we saw two narrow beds in each one, made up carefully with rough grey navy blankets. The outside gardening was casual; that green sword grass that seems to grow anywhere, some aloe vera, and dusty, sprawling, periwinkle. The place was deserted.

We walked along dirt paths lined with whitewashed brick and stone and came out on a mowed patch of grass. On it six or eight people in sunclothes, enjoying the sea air. They greeted us civilly and put away their activities, their books and checkers, to tell us what they knew about the clinic. Contreras, they said, came by in the morning to give his patients a shot of laetril and some enzymes. Patients were told not to smoke or drink. The yoghurt was awful; Mexicans didn't know how to make it. But the worst thing down here was boredom. There was nowhere, really, to go in this new part of town, except the bullfights and the beach. "Sometimes," a woman in her twenties said, "I could *die* for a night at Caesar's and six or eight margaritas."

The others laughed. "Better not," another woman said. But the "I" amazed me. It must have shown on my face. "I have cancer," the young woman, who was wearing a halter top and shorts, gently assured me.

"So do I."

"Me too."

"We all do."

They tried to put us at our ease. All of them had had their operations and their chemotherapy. Their hair had fallen out and grown back in. They were here now.

"Do, do you think . . . this will work?"

From somewhere, the way it almost always did in Mexico, music began to float in the harsh, perfectly tuned air.

"We couldn't know that, could we? And if it doesn't work out, it doesn't matter all that much." That's what a woman in her fifties said, thin and tan, dressed in a loose shirt made from unbleached muslin.

"Is the treatment expensive?" I asked, for the world had said the elusive Contreras was a quack, and hadn't Steve McQueen himself died an awful death down here?

''The hotel is $135 a week, double occupancy. The shots are about twenty. The food is extra. But Mexican food is usually cheap.''

''We like to do most of our shopping at the grocery,'' the girl in the halter top said. ''It gives us ways to spend our mornings.''

My children and I left and drove a mile or so out to the coast. We checked out the beach, and the salt spray, and the fires burning in halved trash cans, the *churros* frying in deep fat, the seared corn on sidewalk grills, the ragtag *mariachis*, the million little kids, the parked cars with a dozen people in them talking. The sea wind blew our hair across our faces.

My father, of course, rejected all suggestions that he go down across the border and take the juice of almond pits into his system. This was his *life* we were discussing. So they took his lung. They gave him a zillion-dollar scan that his insurance paid for. They gave him chemotherapy and radiation and his hair fell out. They tied him to a wheelchair and left him in terror of that imagined China-man, Ching Chang Phooie, who waited, cleaver in hand, until he might try to wheel himself into the bathroom. Walking the halls of the University Hospital, we saw others—Americans accepting the miracles of modern science—sitting on the edges of their beds, slippered feet dangling, propped up in bed, bald as rocks, their wigs slung up on hooks beside them, all of them watching television.

I was afraid of cancer and of dying alone. But what I was really afraid of was what I'd do when and if the kindly doctor sat me down in his tasteful office and gave me that news: Would I choose quonset huts and checkers and *mariachis* and the beach, or would I just totally *go for it*: the chrome, the sonar, the scanners, the boiled food on the tray, the nausea, the false words, the bad faith, the betrayal, the physical agony, the wig on the hook?

When I was a child, America dropped that bomb. Both my cousin and I were tortured by recurrent dreams. I don't know what she saw, but I saw the blast. And tried, *tried*, to get away from its flashing path. Even as a kid I knew that you couldn't hose down your house from radioactive fallout, because where I lived the slightest quake turned off our water. Los Angeles was a desert to begin with, where would the water come from? Later I had my doubts when UCLA designated as a fallout shelter an area enclosed on two sides with sheets of plate glass.

As I grew up and started—how can I say it delicately?—''fooling around,'' I began to notice the soulful concern the men I knew lavished on their dicks, especially when they weren't working properly. Then, as a young wife, married for a second time to a man who had been married before, I watched (simultaneously) Khrushchev on television, banging his shoe in a pet, and my husband, morosely peering down, recalling in an Australian accent that his first wife had tabbed him ''smaller than average.''

Remembering, then, that the Russians are red (and swollen), I realized quite early that the rhetoric wasn't rhetoric; that the sixties plea to ''make love, not war'' was not off the point but exactly on it: to make love often enough that premature ejaculation would finally and absolutely be out of the question.

And to my eyes, at least, though our leaders all spoke of payloads and big bangs and each missile perfectly mimicked a prick right down to the foreskin, nobody cared to *discuss* it. But I had felt, personally, very strongly, from the first time one of my dates misfired, that the world was truly doomed; that there was no hope for us.

Let me see if I can place it in a cool equation. I had heard all my life that ''California'' was irrational. How could I dare to say that it was not? But as a woman, and having seen, all my adult life, grim-lipped men jerking at their missiles, having watched the debacles of poor lost orphan men after their fifth martini, pretending it *was* the fifth martini, and having seen their aimless horrid rage when the stuff dripped out of them: having *that*, as I say, designated by default as "rational," I suppose there was a conspiracy of brain cells on my part to say that maybe there was something else; death's opposite. Not that boring, bearded God who with his thunderbolts and general wrath was just as worried about his payload as our Secretary of Defense himself, but death's *opposite*.

And if women are opposite to men, and California with its easy money and easy ways was opposite to the fierce, demanding East, maybe Lorna, maybe even that loony faggot in the white linen suit . . . they were opposite to something. Maybe they were on to it.

But here's the other side! What if, when Lorna had cleared David Mandlebaum's sinuses thirty years ago, when that shambling concrete university was still no more than a half-dozen mushroom huts, she did it simply by the force of the blow itself? What if Denise's ankle healed in five weeks that time because she was strong and lived in a happy home? What if, in the delicious violet twilight in that Brentwood home across the miniature creek from the Kingdom of Gregory Peck, that skinny kid had done nothing more than twist his arm underneath him? What if those four or five serene people south of the border reading and playing checkers in the mild sun died horrible deaths soon after?

What if our Secretary of Defense and his counterparts, flustered and in their pj's (except the Russians' pajamas were striped, smelly and ill-fitting), really were finally going to end the argument by sticking it to the world with their larger-than-average rockets?

HAVE I SAID ALL THE FEARS? NOT BY A LONG SHOT. THE fear when your child lies sick, fevered—that's a bad one.

The fear of bankruptcy. Just no more money. That quake. The earth finally just deciding that it's *had* it and irritably tossing its crust, and all of us, like fleas, sailing away into infinity. But that other. . . . We all knew it; we all had it. Men went on long stationary bike rides to save their hearts, forgetting—not choosing to remember, to realize that in months—days—their hearts would explode against their poor ribs, their ribs would rub away into the chalk dust of our universe. And women—poor things!—enrolled in estate seminars, forgetting, not *knowing* that there would be no more estates, no more plans. Companies, corporations, joined in. They put the faces, names and histories of missing children on labels and milk cartons, ran columns on them in the paper. Didn't they know? Ah! Of *course* they knew! And wanted all families to be united when. . . .

But there is a terrible strain in uniting the known and the unknown. We know that even now. We really couldn't bring ourselves to *believe* it. Do we believe it now? Sometimes I wake up. I open my eyes: I smell trees, I see stars or clouds, I hold on to . . . Skip. I count, not to three, but to numbers with three and four digits before I remember who I am and where I am and why I'm here. So sometimes it takes a while. And all the way along it's hard to remember exactly what you're afraid of, what we all were afraid of.

By early summer, sometimes I thought that it was all delusion. I thought we were safe. I *knew* we were safe. How could we have worked so hard, in our patch of (what ex-hippies called) our planet, and not have it be safe? Didn't we, all of us, more or less, believe in God? Hadn't everything we'd learned told us that if we worked hard and headed west, that we'd be safe?

One night, in May of 1987, Skip and I were invited to a party at the home of an industrial film producer. In this sweet home, all was family photographs, and homemade ice cream, churned by the man of the house, and the space where a grand piano used to be, until it had been given away to a deserving charity as a tax writeoff: oriental rugs, white walls, yards of zinnias and marigolds put in by the man and woman who lived there, instead of servants: They said there had been ''a deadline'' for the party, but I knew it was because they'd loved to go out back and put flowers in the dirt.

What a lovely party it was. And how dignified we were! The hostess in an organza ruff that came up to her youthful and determined jaw. And all kinds of couples, happily married, chatting and eating catered food. So we were OK. We were perfectly safe. I ask you?! Didn't we have to be safe? I ask you, wherever you were then—in Indiana, lining up at the Dairy Queen; in Beloit, Wisconsin, driving out to watch the lights of the A&W Root Beer stand reflected on the river. If you were in New York City, in that genital softness of May and June, didn't you know, in your heart, that we were safe? Except. . . .

Except later on in the night—I confess I'd had a few white wines—I found myself talking to, being talked at, by a very beautiful woman who'd made a study of the right brain: ''Yes, I go into people's homes,'' she said to me. ''We work all day. I try to put them into some kind of touch with their right brains, their intuitions, their visions, their attachments, their fears.''

''Their *fears*?'' I said. I put my left elbow up on the mantelpiece. There was no fire, but a lot of bric-a-brac was suddenly in jeopardy. ''Listen,'' I said. ''I'm scared. I'm scared of a war.'' I looked around, but no one was listening. ''A war, you know? I think . . . I think it would be so easy for all of it to . . . gee, I don't know. For all of it to just . . .''

The right-brain specialist *was* beautiful, but personally I found her very depressing.

''My father died of cancer,'' I told her. ''The last time I saw him he was wearing a hospital gown, and it was up to his shoulders, and he was jacking off, and crying. He'd been scared to death for weeks before that. He thought there were Chinese gangs after him.''

''That can be. . . .'' She blinked. ''That shows a great many things.''

''I've been married twice. I know that doesn't count for much in these days. But one of those divorces was my fault. I've got two children. They aren't children any more. One of them. . . .''

Truthfully, I'm not sure what I said to her that June night. I know that my fears were no different from the fears of all our friends. The war. First our sons, then our cities. Then ourselves.

Her eyes were wide. She gazed at me with terrific concentration. ''Yes,'' she said, ''I understand what you're saying. I get it. But isn't it true—that your fear of nuclear war is a metaphor for all the *other* fears that plague us today?''

My mind has never been exactly fine. But sometimes it has been good. *''No,''* I said. I may have shouted it out through the beautiful, sheltered room. ''It's *my* view that the other fears, all those of which we have spoken, are a metaphor for my fear of nuclear war!''

She stared at me incredulously, but was spared the difficulty of a response when we were all called in to a very pleasant late supper.

HOW MEN LIVED

JUNE 1987

SOMETIMES I WONDER WHY, IN THE STORIES I TELL NOW, I deal with men so unfairly. It's all how *women* felt, never how men felt, and the implication is, of course, they don't feel. Which may be absolutely right; perhaps they didn't feel. Before I dared to think of banking, or stories either, when I was just a kid in my first marriage to my handsome artist husband, we were once house guests in the home of another handsome artist. It was a small house, a cold house; so damp that it was possible to lie in bed—a mattress and innerspring right down on the floor, naturally—and watch the plaster wall tremble and tingle and then, *pop*, there would be the head of a worm, who, over a period of fifteen minutes or so, would make the trying journey through the wall into the comparative warmth of our almost wet and not very clean sheets, because it was *really* cold outside in the Japanese nursery next door.

And one night there was an art historian there, red-haired, white-faced, flabby, repulsive. He ate boiled rice and vanilla ice cream, and he said he didn't think there were any good women writers. But, I said, what about Carson McCullers? He said he didn't think of Carson McCullers as a writer. But, I said, what about Virginia Woolf? And he said he didn't think of Virginia Woolf as a woman.

It was things like that that made women like me finally ignore men, or how they felt, or what they did. Because listen to some of the things that that man, just that one flabby man, did. He read an article somewhere that smoking increased your sex appeal, and from then on, when you walked by his office, you couldn't see him for the cloud of smoke. He loved ice cream so much that when he went into Baskin-Robbins he came out with a three-scoop ice cream cone, but he had one of those in each hand, six different kinds, managing, in one run, to sample almost twenty percent of the fabled thirty-one flavors. He'd had a wife once who had early on established control by insisting that he do the nightly dishes— why, I ask you, since there were only two of them, didn't they just *go out?* But no, I see him in my mind's eye, standing at the sink, aproned, swabbing out glasses . . .

Of course she left him for another guy. So the poor fool took to watching the other guy's house, and one night went in through the unlocked back door, stopped in the kitchen to pick up a butcher knife, went into the bedroom, presumably to find his wife with her legs locked around her lover's neck and slash them both into shish kebob. Instead, he found two perfect strangers in bed. He sat down on the quilt with those two alarmed strangers, put his head in his hands, and mumbled, "You don't know what I've been through," and told them his story. One last thing. There was a wedding reception once where he was a guest, and, seeing him hovering by the wedding cake looking for a chance to fill his plate with a fifth or sixth helping, my artist-husband said to him maliciously, "The *leaves* are the best part, Phil." Before his mind could make the necessary synapse, process the information that the leaves were in fact gilt paper, Phil's hand had snapped out, snatched a glittering cardboard branch, and stuffed it down his gullet.

But here's the deal! I once heard that art historian speak of me—not unkindly—and describe me as a "bright girl."

So I suppose it was things like that that made me leave men out of my stories.

But—as you've already noticed!—what else besides men did we ever talk about? About the man from Stanford law school who took out Fran O'Donnell and bound and gagged her before he (all too quickly) did it? Or the guy who couldn't decide and couldn't decide whether he really wanted my old friend Lorraine and made such scenes over a period of six or seven months (mostly just doing a series of turns on throwing car keys into the underbrush), that the poor girl finally defenestrated herself, but not fatally? Or the movie producer who was a champagne fountain to his friends but who was so fond of saying, "my house, my rules," to his children by a previous marriage when they came to visit that they . . . well, they finally ended up playing by his rules? Or the other movie producer who left his wife for a guy and then came back to his wife and nagged *her* about it, so that her hair turned grey almost overnight? Or the very prominent doctor who chivied his wife until she committed suicide, and everyone felt sorry for him until they remembered that by a strange coincidence his first wife had committed suicide too, but by that time he couldn't be reached for comment, since he'd taken up scuba diving? And I'm leaving out for the sake of brevity all the thousand and one boys and men who left at night and said they'd call and didn't, or, equally tedious, those poor guys who call every half-hour for ten days or ten years.

But let me just ask you this. Did you ever hear, *before* Christ, about a Saint Agnes getting her breasts sawed off and *smiling* about it, and thinking she was getting a free ticket to heaven? Of course not. Women don't think that way. I believe Agnes was simply in the position of a lot of ladies who take some guy's word for it when he says, "Good night, you were wonderful, and I'll call you tomorrow." Some tomorrow!

And I never heard of a woman anywhere who would eat a

wooden stick with paper leaves on it because the person next to her said it was the best part of the cake! And I never heard a lady say she didn't like men writers because she didn't think of Shakespeare as a writer and she didn't think of Hemingway as a man!

Which is why, although we talked about men all the time, it was only about how they threw up in the rock garden, or never unpacked their trunk when they went to live with Lynda or Jennifer, or how sometimes they *were* very generous and bought unflawed diamonds for their wives, or were "saints" (as demeaning a term in its own way as "swine," because it implied that goodness had descended on them the way appetite descended on poor Phil when he snapped out his hand to pluck gritty paper leaves off white icing and made them disappear into his mouth).

So, get it? We talked about men all the time, but they didn't figure in our stories.

But they have to go into the story, because aren't they the ones who did it? Didn't they make the world we were living in? Weren't they the ones driving the train?

In June of 1987, the vice-president of my bank spent three straight weeks at the track and came out about an eleven-hundred-dollar winner. The governor got a haircut. Men drank in bars, hit their wives, made love to their women friends, explained to their children that there was a God. Some built shelters. Everybody had a theory; nobody had a good one. Priests gave their best sermons. My own feeling is that, in general, men all across the northern hemisphere suffered grave humiliation, a humiliation that went far, far beyond despair or fear. It was as though in the great on-going dick-waving contest of all the centuries before us and the centuries to come, someone else was definitively going to win.

Men talked and wrote a lot, but they kept their lives a secret. When they said something, you most often could take that as a key: It wasn't true.

This is what I think a man I knew might have done before the end. Not my first husband, Jack, because he, along with a girlfriend, climbed up into the Rocky Mountains to live in a tent. Not my second husband, Dirk, because he went back to Australia, his island home (but still wrote once a week, asking Denise to ''come out''). Not Hal, my silly prince, not my dear friend, Skip. Just a *man*, you know? Someone I knew. Someone like I used to go out with. I use him only because maybe there's a Chinaman's chance, not of figuring out what he thought but of saying what he did. I promise nothing, certainly not that this will be a story.

HE WOKE UP. SWEATING. HE'D BEEN RUNNING IN HIS SLEEP. His wife's hand was on his shoulder. His dreams had been full of blood, screaming, axes. Running, either toward or away from all of it. His son's face, reproaching him. He has to piss, so he grunts, heaves out of bed, goes in the half-dark, bangs up the seat, pees noisily. Wonders about his prostate. Remembers he has a friend, *had* a friend, with cancer of the prostate. Shakes his dick. Shakes drops of urine on the wall. Starts back to bed. Detours to the kid's room. The kid has kicked off the covers and lies on his stomach, his fist in his mouth. The walls of the room, barely visible in the dark, covered with pennants and posters from the Dodgers, Knicks, Rams, Kings.

So he goes back. Gets into bed. ''Spoons'' with his wife. Puts his hand over on her stomach. She pushes it away. He moves his hand to her breast. Then both breasts. She sighs. He takes that to mean she's awake. She is awake. His dick hardens. He sticks it in. She doesn't mind. All this time his mind has been . . . somewhere else. Remembering the blood and shouting from his dream. Now that's blotted out by . . . waves that fan out from the base of his spine to his solar plexus, sometimes as far down as his knees, but mostly his dick, rubbing it against the place where her twat is closest to

her asshole. He feels rather than hears the sigh in her. Thinks
next time he'll do the "right thing," turn her over, pay attention to what *she* wants, etc., but, Christ sake, it's four in
the morning, what does she *want*? Comes, and in those five
draining seconds, recalls that there may not be too many next
times, if they're serious about all this, remembers the white
blond head over there in the next room, becomes that helpless kid himself, buries his head in his wife's patient but
unresponsive neck, and her patience and unresponsiveness
comfort him; he sleeps, plunges into it.

He wakes up, on his back. The kid, his Masters-of-the-
Universe pajamas wet and foul-smelling, sits across him.
"Don't you ever..!" he crankily begins, but blots out the
sentence, loses himself in throwing the boy up in the air.
Again and again he tosses the kid. First the kid plants his
feet on his stomach (flat and hard as ever!). Then he takes
the kid, holds him by his waist, pulls him up over his head—
the kid holding himself straight, so that they're parallel. He
uses the kid as weights, lowering him so that their chests
almost touch, then extends his arms, pushes the kid away.
The kid loves it, giggling, but holding rigid, remembering
to do his part.

Then he does the same thing with his feet; does leg lifts
with the kid. His own feet, though small, reach from the
kid's hips almost to his collarbone. The kid, going up farther
away now, looks apprehensive. He extends his legs, extends
them, bends them, bends them, begins to grunt. It's hard
work, but he's in shape. He loses the time. Remembers it.
Loses it. Loses it again.

"Come on. Breakfast's ready."

He drops the boy (who whines about it), slouches into the
kitchen. He likes to eat alone. His breakfasts, over the years,
have been a source of contention. Raw liver and tomato juice
with his first wife. Raw potatoes and olive oil with his second. He likes oatmeal now, but he doesn't like to think about
it. Doesn't want to be bugged about it. His wife has been

listening to the morning news, and her face is the color of a slug's.

"Turn it off," he says. "The kid needs changing. Are you going to change him or what?"

She looks like she wants to talk, but he looks like he *doesn't* want to talk. So there it is. She goes into the other room and he hears her soft voice, chastising and cajoling the boy.

It's only about eight, a cloudy day. He mostly doesn't go in to the office until ten, then stays until six-thirty or seven, and works late a couple of times a week. So now he suits up. His running clothes are out in the double garage where his wife last ran them through the washer. (Or, he guesses she did.) He puts them on, laces his shoes, goes out the garage's side door, loping. Down the sidewalk, the ocean visible about four blocks away and down the hill; he doesn't notice it. When he was young, first married, still in college, it seemed like he never went to classes but left (a smaller house than this) every day and went down about this time to the great rolling breakers and had a beer or two with his friend Buzz. They poured some beer out of every bottle onto the sand: *"Eh, Poseidon!"* and body-surfed most of the rest of the day. Read all night. Drank and practiced bullfighting passes out in the street. Got divorced. Picked fights. Did some hunting. All that stuff.

Now he mildly runs; a middle-aged man. By strokes of luck most of his old friends are dead, their wives "gone on to brighter subjects," out of the country or on to new marriages. The ghosts of his dead friends . . . even those he served with in Vietnam tickle his brain. If it *is* death coming, he barely thinks, big deal. Didn't Bill do it already? Didn't Buzz, with his dreams of being a bullfighter, and his girlfriend who loved him so much she killed herself after he died? There's a glamour to it . . .

The houses are handsome, the ones he runs by, but he doesn't notice. He listens to himself breathe, he feels his pulse, he feels the blood and muscle in his body. His body is like a beanbag, stretched tight with beans.

He runs five miles, through the Pacific Palisades. People ignore him. He ignores them.

He comes back in through the garage side door, strips his clothes off onto the top of the washer, walks naked in through the kitchen to the bathroom. The kid is eating oatmeal, his wife sits on a high kitchen stool, talking on the telephone to someone; she puts her hand over the speaker as he passes by.

He showers. And dresses, in good slacks, perfectly ironed shirt, jacket, no tie. His car, a BMW, coughs before starting. He swears. He's a few minutes late. He irritably presses the electric garage opener, presses it again. The door slides away, he guns the motor, skids out the driveway, jams the car into first, sees his wife's pale face at the front window; he's neglected to say goodbye. He waves her away, turns his face away, drives away.

He pulls into the think tank where he works. They work mostly on nonsecurity things now. (Or, they're "defensive," not offensive; soft, not hard.) Where do they store the antibiotics? Should the government stockpile tranquilizers? What about the pill that keeps radioactivity out of the thyroid gland? Also, what about terrorism? What about looting? What about plague? Twenty-two deaths in New Mexico alone so far this year; the year's only half over, and nothing has even "happened" yet. Government grants, reports every few weeks or months. Nobody does anything.

And nobody here thinks anything's going to happen, so the atmosphere is a lot more peaceful than at home, where his wife is about to wet her pants. The guard "records" him in. He flashes his pass and walks down the long neon-lit hall, saying howzit goin' about a hundred and fifty times until he gets to his office. His secretary has called in sick. Sick, shit! His stomach turns with contempt at the chickenheartedness of women.

But then he sits down, looks at the report he's doing, a syllabus on L.A.'s twelve major hospitals and the fifty-two minor ones and where they're going to get their electricity in case an "earthquake" might happen.

Well, what the fuck does *he* care where they're going to get their fucking electricity!

He looks at the plants—creeping charlies—hanging from his ceiling. They're in top shape. He calls his buddy, Chas, his sole surviving buddy from the old days, but Chas is teaching a class, won't be back for an hour. He looks at the phone. Sighs. Dials Jennifer.

"Oh! Oh! I was praying you'd call, call just once before . . . before . . ."

"You know we can't see each other again," he says. "You know we agreed to that. It would kill my wife."

Jennifer's already begun to cry.

"Why aren't you at work?" he says crossly. "What are you doing at home anyway?"

"I'm afraid," she says.

"Well, *shit!*" And within minutes he hangs up. But he doesn't feel exactly unhappy.

At eleven-thirty he dials another number. "What are you wearing?" he says, instead of hello.

"What do you *think* I'm wearing?"

"I mean, are you wearing a decent dress? Pantyhose? Like that?" His voice has taken on a pleasing, light quality.

"I'm wearing my blue silk, and a white linen blazer. What are *you* wearing?"

"Wanna go to lunch at Jimmy's?"

"Jimmy's? When?"

She's considering. He knows she has a lunch date, she always does. She's three inches taller than he is, long blond hair, pretty brown legs. He hasn't nailed her, yet.

"Today. Now." He smiles into the phone. "Soft-shelled crab? Before they go out of season."

"I'll call you back."

And just as he's beginning to lose hope, she does.

So there they are, at Jimmy's, in beautiful Beverly Hills; one o'clock, the height of the lunch hour. Every customer a face from a defunct television series. He holds her arm above the elbow, he pushes her slightly in front of him to a (not very good) table. They order soft-shell crab, it's delicious, and end up with three champagne cocktails each. Utter safety, utter luxury. They banter. She reminds him that he's married. He says, "So? It's the end of the world! Do you think they have divorce courts in heaven?"

"Or alimony?" she counters, drily, since no one can be sure the end is coming; the general feeling here in Jimmy's is that at least it won't be coming until after lunch.

She says no, she's fond of him, he's cute, he's always been cute, but he's married, and she doesn't want that on her conscience. He idly pulls out a notepad from his inside jacket pocket and begins drawing stick figures of animals, only a *nice* man draws stick figures of animals. On another small, separate page, he writes out, "You're a lion and a cheetah, the lynx of which I never gnu." His handwriting is straight, honest, stylish. She laughs. She sees right through him. They order raspberries, and suddenly he knows it; he knows he's going to score. "Had we but world enough and time," he says lightly, "this coyness, lady, were no crime," and in his mind he blesses the professor from his past who insisted that each of them learn a poem before they got out of English survey.

The words are truer than he even means, and she looks at him with something more now. He remembers the first stuff about beautiful breasts, and "vegetable love." He leaves out the lines in the middle about death, except for the part about the grave being a fine and private place. Then he says, fairly loud and very clear, "Let us roll all our strength and all our sweetness, up into one ball, and tear our pleasures with rough strife, through the iron gates of life. Thus, though we cannot make our sun stand still, yet we can make him run."

He's *out* of himself, suddenly. He knows the guy's right, he remembers that when Marvell was alive things were just about as iffy as they are now, and yet those guys went on, and life went on. He looks at her, so young, so blond, so tan, so fresh, and he remembers his own friends, so *dead* by now, right down to that Mark Del Vecchio, dead on a curve driving home, and he thinks of his first two wives with their sensible haircuts and wrinkles beginning in their necks, their "careers," and he takes her hand and says, "So, OK. Are we going to bed? Because I really want to."

And her face flushes, he can actually see fine sweat break out across her smooth forehead. "Yes," she says, and he smiles. "I won't settle for anything less." It's already an old joke between them.

He excuses himself, makes reservations in a bungalow of the Bel Air Hotel. They drive, laughing, excited, and then they're there, sneaking in, giggling, giddy, waiting impatiently for room service to bring champagne, and he has the presence of mind to pay for all of it in cash, so that the credit chits won't find their way home.

And she's beautiful. And moved. Won't let him go. There's a sincerity in her lovemaking that spurs him on. Since this morning took the edge off, he can stay hard forever, *and* manages to come twice. Not bad for a forty-two-year-old. They talk between and after. Or she talks; he puts an interested look on his face and just watches her, her flat stomach, perfect breasts; pays no attention to what she says about her first husband, her son at home. Suddenly she turns to him again, locking tan arms around his neck; he hears muffled sobs in there someplace. *Hell*, he doesn't want that. Gently (he thinks), he reminds her he has to get home. He is, as he reminds her, a married man.

He drives her to her car, kisses her tenderly, says he'll call her the next day, can't read her expression. She *can't* want more from him. Or is she waiting impatiently for him to leave? Put it this way—does she have another date for to-night? Is she a nymphomaniac? He only feels fatigue.

He goes back to the office, calls Chas, tells him about it, but in an indifferent, offhand way that suggests he has trouble at home and despair in his life, so what *else* can he do? Then they talk about the sex, and laugh. The laughing inspires him. "Whadyasay we go to the game tonight?" Chas says his wife'll give him hell, and he's got papers to correct, and *he* doesn't have time to fuck all day and play all night, but then says sure.

So then he calls his wife and says Chas just called, and he's got tickets for the game. He can barely hear her. For a minute he's worried; she should get out more, is that it? Because, as he says to her with exasperation, if the world's ending there's not a damn thing anybody can do about it, doesn't she understand that? She says a lot of people are leaving, she's heard about it on the news, and he says for Christ's sake, doesn't she understand, the news people get *paid* for reporting bad news, does she think *good* news sells cereal?

There's silence, broken-hearted and stubborn. He sighs, says, "Look. You want me to come home then?" And the thing is, it isn't just a game; he *is* worried about her.

"No," she says.

So then it's back into the car after signing out and driving downtown on the Santa Monica Freeway. It's a sellout game at Dodger Stadium, he's paid fifty dollars apiece for these tickets from a private agency and used up the last of his Mastercharge. He meets Chas at Tai Hong in Chinatown. They have a few beers, leave one car there, and wait until the first half of the first inning is over before they make the last fifteen-minute push up the Chavez Ravine hill, because the truth is, neither one of them is that crazy about baseball. They talk, laugh, kick back.

Nobody here is worried.

That's a fact.

He feels a smile splitting his face, with a beer in one hand and a hot dog in the other, and some asshole behind him whose one comment seems to be, "Back to the farm!" when someone he doesn't like comes up to bat. The trees on the far side of the stadium, Chavez Ravine, look like they've been painted. Or, they look like the thousand-piece jigsaw he had as a kid.

Afterward they chow down some noodles at Tai Hong, and Chas drives home.

Then there he is in Chinatown at ten-thirty at night, with a lot of Chinamen giving him looks like, "Didn't I hear your mother calling you? Isn't it time for you to go home?" But boy! he sure doesn't want to go home.

He goes back inside to the phone booth. He calls Jennifer. She answers after one ring and weeps to hear him. He tells her he was thinking about her; he hates to hurt her, but she's got to get over him. She says she'll never get over him. He says she must. She begins crying again and says can't she just see him once? She reminds him, with an edge in her voice, *he* called her. She takes this to mean he still has some affection for her too. His prick, old fire horse, jerks its head, then falls back.

No, he says sharply, doesn't she realize he's a married man? She hangs up.

Furious, he begins to dial again, then dials the number of the tan beauty he's spent the afternoon with. A man answers, and he, of course, hangs up.

He has to smile. Maybe she's just invited that guy up for some Harvey's Bristol Cream. Forget it.

Forget it.

Driving home, he puts on tapes of Mexican music: *Que Lindo Es Jalisco, Cascabel.* He can't help it; he thinks of his dead friend Buzz, the fun they used to have, the killer despair that was behind it even then. Body surfing, for instance; the ease, the thrust, the gliding, and then the sharp mistake. You got thrown and pounded, guys broke their necks that way.

The sharp stones and shells, the breathlessness, the plain coldness of the water, and the heat of the sun, and the laughing, and the hookey-playing from the wives who, it turned out, were doing a little hookey-playing of their own—but under all of it, through it, an oil slick of despair. He remembers how Marya, Buzz's Latvian girlfriend, would come into the Foreign Club, down in Tijuana late at night, and she'd have some greaser on her arm, prepared to pay. She'd throw down a couple of fifties and say, "Make them play me some *music*, Buzz!"

He feels tears sting as he listens to those tapes: *Que Lindo Es Jalisco!* How beautiful, Jalisco, how beautiful. So beautiful that even when you *got* there, you never really got there . . . His eyes sting for the two blond kids he and Buzz used to be, so *up* for it; so in love with those blondes they were always chasing, so crazy for the music and the surf . . . But another, sour, part of his mind remembers that his particular blonde gained a cool thirty-five pounds and took to calling him in the middle of the night after he was married to a whole other wife, and that Buzz got to be a tiresome drunk, bringing out his bullfighting cape not even after but *during* dinner parties, baiting an imaginary *toro* in the streets, and asking rhetorically, "Where have all the dreams gone? Where?"

And that was fifteen years ago.

He pulls up in front of his house. Two stories, set back, nice front lawn, magnolia in front. Exasperated, he sees they haven't fastened the gate to the back. Anybody could come in.

He's been married three times, and if he lets himself think about it, they're all the same woman. How could he have done that? He knows *she's* up there, probably awake, and well aware of how long ago the game ended. He thinks of Chas and how his first wife wanted to leave him so badly she drove away in the family car even though she didn't know how to drive.

He eases the car into the garage, locks everything up, goes

by the inside door to the kitchen, automatically opens the refrigerator, and takes out a beer. It's close to one o'clock; he's wide awake. He's brought in his briefcase—he sits at the dining room table in the dark for a few minutes, then sighs, goes over to the light switch, turns it on, blinks, squints, opens his briefcase, goes out and makes himself a sandwich—even though he isn't hungry—forgets to clean up, begins to look at the data for the report.

What a bunch of bullshitters! All these hospitals, the small ones especially, live off insurance and thieves who pass for doctors. All of them would croak for a government grant. So all of them say they're "perfectly prepared" for "any emergency," and some of them get coy about "thick concrete walls," even though they know that if the so-called emergency they're talking about really *was* an earthquake they'd all be squashed like roaches under those thick concrete walls . . . He decides to write more of an exposé instead of a report, and if they don't like it, fuck it. He just can't stand the lying.

He focuses in on five separate hospitals he knows for a fact are either abortion mills or specialize in nose jobs and *then* focuses in on their private generators—their size, possible wattage, location. The truth is, their private electrical systems wouldn't hold up in a high wind, and they know it.

He moves from that to their food supply. Given the size of the hospitals, and the square footage of their storage capacity, there's just no *way* they could be stocking the food stores they should be stocking. He flashes on his wife, pale and crazed, walking the aisles of the local supermarket, looking anxiously at cans, buying things like *sacks* of pinto beans and her bottled water that she frets over, knowing it won't last in plastic, God knows, and glass will break, but how are you going to cook a pinto bean (or *live*, come to think of it) without water?

And so he goes to water supply and storage, and, of course, none of the smaller hospitals have it, they haven't even *thought* about it in a couple of cases. He's able to write a fifteen-page first draft that will set them on their *ears* over there before his wife comes down and says since it's after four in the morning, why doesn't he come to bed?

It's what he's been waiting for. He informs her she's not his mother and he'll come to bed when he wants. He tells her it's a good thing that the end of the world she's so worried about really *isn't* coming, because God knows nobody around here is doing a damn thing about it, and she whispers that the Vospers went down today and got their passports. But he escalates and says there's nowhere, *nowhere in the world* anyone can hide, and how can she be fool enough not to know that? And if he hears a satirical second voice whispering in his brain, a voice from off that old record from the sixties (or even the fifties), a lot of English crackpots satirizing the end of the world, intoning, "*Will This Wind*?!" he ignores it and shrieks at her to have some courage, to stand up to—not just her fate, but *the human condition*! Can't she get it through her head that she won't be the only one to die but that all of Western civilization will soon be an ash, a cinder?

She opens her mouth to an oval, in such a way that he believes she might be saying *Australia* or *Argentina,* and he roars at her that the only way to live is to *live! Carpe Diem! Seize the Day!* Live all of it all the way up! Fear isn't going to solve anything! And finally he sees fear in her face modulate into boredom and dislike.

"Can't you keep your voice down?" she asks, which she must know by now is not the way to get him to keep his voice down. He goes into a reprise of "To His Coy Mistress" with the theme this time that unless you have known, truly known, life, you are doomed to be forever afraid of death. His voice takes on resonance, he's yelling at all his wives by now; all the brown mice he's ever married.

By now her expression has turned to frozen scorn, but there's an air of waiting about her; she's waiting for a cue, and so he cranks it up a little: As a light goes on next door, he makes sure to lecture her on love *and* God. If she really believed in God she wouldn't be afraid of what came next in this Great Adventure we call Life and then, *finally*, the little boy appears at the top of the stairs, clutching his teddy and sobbing, and his wife gives her husband a standard killing look and scuttles back upstairs to put the kid to sleep again.

He sighs. Goes out to the kitchen to get another beer. Puts away the sandwich stuff. Pours out the water and grounds for coffee so that she won't have to do it in the morning. Goes upstairs, takes a piss, brushes his teeth. She's already back in bed, turned away from him. He gets in, spoons up against her. She allows it. Puts his hand across her breasts. She puts his hand down on her hip. He sleeps.

Now, I CAN SEE ALL KINDS OF THINGS WRONG WITH THAT story.

The first thing I see wrong is: He was only yelling at his wife to drive the fear out of her, to hold it at bay like a circle of wolves in the snow. He knew (I presume, I *know*) that "love" wasn't going to do it, because he didn't love her and she didn't love him; a show of "love" would only make the fear larger, wider, deeper. And it could be argued that he was doing the same thing for the kid as well: If Dad's having a tantrum, what could be bad?

And the second thing I see wrong is that you see that man only from his women. I know, having been a wife, jilted lover, jilting lover, how those guys act with their women. And I know perfectly well what Henry James said about the writer who guessed all about France just by walking by the concierge's apartment when he had the door open; that you can guess the pattern of the rug just by seeing the corner of the rug; but Henry James didn't know anything more about men than I do. (Put another way, he just doesn't seem like a *man* to me, OK?)

And third, if you'll look at that day, that man, you could say a lot of things about him, but you could never say he thought about the "world situation." His war memories, had I seen fit to include them, would be this: His carrier has docked at Manila. Will he be allowed to disembark in order to participate in an all-Pacific track meet and risk death in the 120-degree heat, or will the crusty, half-wit Admiral have his way and make him peel potatoes or—I forget the rest of the story. Or will he try to enlist in (let's say World War II) and he's six feet one and weighs only 135 pounds, but the Navy says, "We want your mind, not your body!" Only it turns out they don't want his body *that* much! Or, he might be a morose, heavy-drinking clerk-typist up in Newfoundland, called upon to explain where the company has mislaid a bright orange, $52,000 earth-mover that has inexplicably been heisted? Or he could be a paunchy misfit whose jocular motto is: "*I* go after the women and children go!" Or he could be a nice man named Bazz Gargulio who goes into the Army infirmary with a bad headache, thinking he needs glasses, and comes to find out he has spinal meningitis, and his friends who aren't allowed to come to visit, break the quarantine by rolling beer cans across the floor to where he lies sweating, saying, boy, does he have a headache!

So the point I'm trying to make is: The men I blamed and ignored and ridiculed and pleaded with didn't have a damn thing to do with it. They . . . were . . . *clueless* as regards the world situation.

So, who *did* do it? Those men who, having invented the atom, had to go to dinner parties with their briefcases strapped to their belts? The man who, when the Nike missile was invented, went around giving talks in front of men's clubs, saying (as crepe-paper streamers floated out behind electric fans), "This, gentlemen, is the NIKE!"? The boy I met once on a Rhine cruise, his hair shaved to peach fuzz and his poor brain the size of the pit that went with it, who said, by way of conversation, *"I just love missiles"*? The Pentagon colonel, close as I ever got to the seat of power, who had rodent genitals and loved Twinkies and Snowballs, pink Snowballs, better than all the golden caviar and champagne in the Western world?

What I'm getting at is, what if *nobody* did it, really? What if the Secretary of War himself was just as scared as the wife in my story? What if the people who made nerve gas truly *never* got it into what lived under their hair that if you threw some of that stuff at a Communist, he'd turn to green jelly like a jade tree in a killing frost, and actually up and die?

That would square with what I know of "men," those shouting red-faced loonies who howl that "you can't have it both ways," even as they're dancing to a tune that lets *them* have it both ways, *three* ways, if they can get it up long and hard enough; those irate, broken-home fathers who keep their kids in line by droning "My house, my rules!" even as they wait anxiously for the results of this week's gonorrhea test; those husbands who get their feelings hurt when they feel their horns pushing out, even as they peruse the hotel's gift shop for plum-colored G-strings for this afternoon's beloved.

But what I want to know is: Who *did* think up the gas that goes on your skin and you throw up into your gas mask (if you have one) until you strangle on your vomit? It must have been a guy somewhere. Why don't we know his name? Do *men* know his name, just like they always know the name of the Dodgers' new shortstop? The secretary of the man who invented the vomiting gas must have known something, or did she just think of him as the generous lover who bought her the nightgown with the silver threads in grey chiffon and the matching negligee with the white feathers at the neck, or the cruel lover who stopped asking if she'd like to forget this world with him at the Beverly Hilton or the Foghorn down at the Marina? Maybe his wife knew he was a salamander, a newt, a subhuman who never should have crawled up out of the slime, but still she had to worry that he didn't spend enough time with the kids.

Or, what do I know? Maybe he spent all the time in the *world* with his kids, and planted tuberous begonias, and went down on his wife for hours at a time, and never even *looked* at another woman, and knew all the lyrics to "A Capital Ship for an Ocean Trip" and "Oh, That Strawberry Roan!" I mean, it's possible. All I know, for sure, is that men were the most beautiful and exalted creatures in the world; the funniest and, I'm willing to say, maybe the closest to God. Or they could have been before they fell.

I just don't know any stories about them. Any stories that ring true, anyway.

PARADISE

THERE WERE DAYS IN THE SUMMERTIME WHEN EDITH woke up and the day was absolutely perfect. The wallpaper was flowered. There was the smell of coffee and bacon. The old-fashioned crank-out windows had been open all night to the bright smell of pepper trees and the sound of that feathery green lace against the iron grilling. Or—if she woke up at her girlfriend Beryl's house—that whole big white room with elaborate ceiling moldings would be glittering to the day; the white organdy curtains fluttering, the sun sedate, cool, even, just bowling up over the horizon. It would be summer after the June fogs and before broiling August days when the fires began in the canyons around the city and it got too hot to be much fun.

It would be the kind of day when even your mothers knew there wasn't much to do. There might be a silly chore like *cleaning out the medicine chest*, taking out the medicines, peering and poking at everything, taking off the lids of jars and sniffing, looking at each other, because you always ended up doing those silly chores together, sniffing at somebody's sinus drops or hemorrhoid ointment. Because we were immortal; thin (without even thinking about it), tan, strong, young. Everything struck us funny. Suppose you saw Beryl's dad's migraine tablets

159

and you struck your forehead with the heel of your hand and made a face—and then you'd be buckled with laughter, breathless with laughter, stifled with laughter, lapsed, lost.

And so it would take you two hours to clean that chest, because part of the time you'd be plucking your eyebrows, or Beryl's eyebrows, or you'd try on her mother's Prince Machebelli and then remember you weren't supposed to get into that and spend ten minutes scrubbing it off your wrists and neck. And then her mother, irritated, inspecting, would find a line of grit on a shelf, some left-over Dutch cleanser, and you'd take out the contents of the shelf again, Beryl starting to sulk and slam things, but then we'd hear her father's voice, complaining to his wife, "Do they have to be so noisy? It's Saturday *morning!*" And at the sound of his voice Edith would pound her head with the heel of her hand.

Oh! the laughter!

By ten-thirty be out of the house. Either you would have "gotten a ride" or you wouldn't have. Usually you walked, for *miles*, drifting in long angles from one side of the sidewalk to another, bumping into each other until you thought to say about yourselves that you were "joined at the hip." You talked about the new slips you would buy, or the angora sweaters you'd get in September, or whether Beryl would get a nose job, or if you put those angoras in the refrigerator at night would they really keep from shedding? They talked: Jerry Nora was cute, Jerry Bridges was *so cute*. Bob McGinty was dangerous! Harry Montana couldn't even *read*! (But he was cute.) They talked about Morgan Morgan. (And the name sent them into a frenzy of laughter.) They talked and talked and finally one of them might break down and say, "That Roger Hill, *he's* . . ." And the other one, it could be Edith or Jackie or Sally or Beryl or Deborah, would give a bump of the hip and say, lilting, "Well? *Cultivate* him!"

Where did those girls walk? They walked for miles in the center of the city, Los Feliz Boulevard, which was like a ribbon park, house upon house with moist lawn tendrils down to the busy road. They walked northeast and down a long sweet incline to where Griffith Park Boulevard and Los Feliz and Fletcher Drive met to form a strange frontier between the neighborhoods of Atwater, Glendale, the "Los Feliz District" and "the Valley"—not the San Fernando Valley but that three-block strip between the hills that sheltered Chavez Ravine and railroad tracks that snaked along, parallel to the hills, into the depths of downtown.

At that junction, of course, were the Griffith Park fountain and, across the street, the Griffith Park swimming pool.

They walked the old streets, Hyperion over to Vermont, stopping at the grocery store at the other "junction"— Sunset and Hollywood Boulevard—and then sometimes walked east along Sunset to see Jackie, where she lived at the base of the Micheltorena Hill, caught in another wide ravine where scrubby Los Angeles hills rose high on either side of them, scrolled along the tops with palms. The houses were shabby.

Or they turned west on Sunset, to Hollywood itself, riding on the "red car," over to the Pantages Theatre, or the Egyptian, or Grauman's Chinese. Or just got off at Vine and *walked* the width of the town they knew, over to La Brea, stopping for hot fudge sundaes at C. C. Brown's and then heading back on the south side, looking at Baker's Shoes, and Joyce's, loitering in the Broadway Hollywood, playing with the costume jewelry. And back on the red car again, and then another long, long walk, home.

They walked out in the industrial sections of Glendale for miles, trying to find the double Bob's Big Boy—the first drive-in to have *two* drive-ins: and doubledecker hamburgers at each one. They walked south again, back down to Fletcher Drive, where next to a trestle between two scraped brown cliffs, a "yellow car" swished periodically by, and just underneath, in the miniature Valley, a long, tall, pink, enormous strawberry cardboard ice cream cone tickled the sky—a replica of Currie's Mile High ice cream cones.

They were always on their way someplace, but in the summer they had all day to get there, and once they got there, was that the place they really wanted to be?

Once, at a children's kiddie park somewhere, four of them got there and found that the place was closed and that anyway they had no money. Jackie sat in a toy train and said *"choo choo!"* Lorraine, who had come to see if the boy who ran the miniature ferris wheel was there, absently bumped against the generator that ran it. "Well, *cultivate!*" Beryl smiled. A single candy stand was open; the man who ran it gave them four cotton candies for the price of one, or for no price at all. Those girls were young, and cute. They didn't need money; they didn't need to pay.

Hour after hour they strolled the deserted kiddie park, staring, eating, jabbering, bumping, laughing, bored beyond all belief, but happy. So happy! Jackie led the way over to the baby-boats sitting in a doughnut-shaped lake, dark green and cool. The girls—who ten years before had been solemn tots, each in her own boat, steering the curves of this ride or another—circled the round pond, trailing their fingers in the dark water. "*Well, kid*, do you think he *might* be there? *Well*, just . . . *smile* at him!" "Oh, I *couldn't!*" "No . . . well . . . you might." "I mean . . .''

Because if you smiled, a boy might materialize out of the rolling crowds in the halls of John Marshall High School, right after second period on a Tuesday morning, and say, *"Hey!* Wanna wear my sweater?", thrust it at you and disappear, because Wednesday was the day the girls got to wear the boys' letterman sweaters. Each Wednesday Edith and every girl she knew dressed prudently in a straight skirt and tailored blouse, because those sweaters looked *awful* over a dress . . . And at three o'clock you'd spot him, somebody named David or Jerry or Phil or "Brugie," circling warily with a dozen or more boys, all in low-slung Levis over perky little hips and perfectly laundered white, long-sleeved shirts, laughing, sneering, combing their hair, then rushing up, and you watched as he peeled off the sweater . . .

"Here's your . . ."

But he'd have vanished. Scooted.

And on Wednesday the same thing happened with the bright satin "Eisenhower" jackets, except that the Y club jackets showed as plainly as Hindu caste marks, rich boys, sad boys, poor boys, bad boys. To wear the royal blue of the Savants was to be blue-eyed, blond, well cared for by good parents. Who cared about the clubs in between? Pale turquoise or lemon yellow, clubs of uncertain repute, but at the other end of the social scale, dark and greasy, the Vandals, made up of boys whose Levis hung by absolutely nothing, defying everything! What had made those bad boys turn into a Y *club?* The jackets of course, kelly green and shiny. Harry Montana was such a bad speller that his embroidered name came out Mantana! On Wednesdays, only Mexican girls with pompadours wore the jackets of the Vandals except for *three weeks once,* when Jackie and Lorraine and Edith were asked to wear those jackets. Those bad boys wafting sweet kisses in their minds onto the shoulders of cotton-candy good blonde girls; the girls feeling forbidden caresses everywhere the jackets touched.

Kisses of the mind.

Jackie, fourteen, never kissed—except during spin-the-bottle—still under the apprehension that you must hold your breath when you kiss, and still serious about that one thing, gets tired of just trailing her hand in the baby-boat water. It's hot, and the sun brings out a mist on the upper lips of all the girls. Their starched, white, freshly ironed, peasant blouses begin to prickle. Then, without missing a beat or a syllable, Jackie, rubbing and bumping up against the boat ride, rucks up her skirt, lifts it dreamily in bunches—she's already barefoot—drapes one pale thigh over the short, bright, metal barricade and suddenly she's *in the water,* still talking: "What do you think *he* said? What did *she* say then?" Drifting as she speaks, from baby-boat to boat, delicately playing with the steering wheels, splaying pale fingers along and across the boats, and then Lorraine, with some giggles and some *ooohs*! is in the water too, except she's shorter, and there's some fear that the water will get all the way to . . .

Beryl laughs, a little uneasy—is there any way her mother will find out?—cautiously steps in, and looks delighted. Then Edith. It's delicious, cool, suspect, soft at the bottom. The candy man looks on, heavy-lidded, and a cloud—a skimpy one—slides across the sun.

The water! What they wanted was to be popular, to laugh, to bump together, to grow up but to stay still, to sit in their mothers' laps and be loved. They wanted to dance at dances, borrow each other's clothes, go to the park, ride the merry-go-round, pick out a grassy hill at Griffith Park, climb to the top and roll down. Then do that again. And again.

This morning, after the medicine chest, they finally get away from Beryl's mother. She definitely does not approve of Beryl's going swimming in a public pool because of polio, so Beryl wears her suit under her clothes as she leaves—they know they're going swimming but they don't know where.

PART 3

I am, and there is nothing outside of me. . . . I am all. I am one, and within me is multiplicity. . . . I am fire. I am chaos. . . . I am God. I am the ineffable bliss of dissolution/ I am the joy of death. . . .

—Alexander Scriabin
The Swiss Notebooks

THE LIGHT AGES

MAY 1987—JULY 1990

Some say it was a Bad Time
But I say it was a Good Time

HERE'S WHAT FRANZ deGELD DID WHEN THINGS BEGAN to look iffy in California—some of this I know first hand, some I picked up from Lorna, some I read in the columns, some I heard from Golden Oaks parents, O.K.?

He went back to his wife, really back.

The way you knew it, people joked about it—was that Scratch Café (that white-painted California cuisine palace that used to be the "Tumble Inn" during the sixties and God knows what else in the years before that) suddenly had its carefully architected interior despoiled by flocks of sobbing starlets, all of whom had signed up to meet Franz and, after some artichoke salad and duck pasta, were looking toward a magic afternoon in his private spa across the street in his glamourous office-studio.

Day after day Franz made dates and then stood them up. Often those girls—dressed to the nines, as we say—had *hitchhiked* or had their mothers drop them off at the far west of the city, down in the bowels of Venice. They went in the restaurant, had one Cinzano, then two, then—what?—realized they couldn't pay for what they'd already ordered, and then began to cry. Nobody knows now how they settled their bills.

Franz took out Australian visas and was on the phone to Sydney and Melbourne all day long; all night long. But he couldn't close any deals. (And also his staff overheard him saying nothing would happen.)

About that time he made a commercial for the telephone company, advising the American public to "keep in touch," just like he did. It's safe to think that all across western America and over on the eastern seaboard, shoes were flung by pretty girls and dapper young boys at Franz's petulant face, framed in luminous Renaissance black, speaking about how he couldn't *live* without calling up his old friends.

This is how Franz spent the day he went home. He woke to cottony coastal fog, so thick it drifted through the coarse-cut screens of his renovated warehouse and into the art deco studio he'd turned into an immensely profitable film factory. He woke in a cloud. Propped up by futons unfolded by minions each night to form a different pattern on the highly polished floor, he opened his eyes to see, scuttling, maybe thirty feet away, a furtive rodent, just the grey tail. Well. Old building.

Too near to him sprawled some girl, Kathleen was it? Kaitlin? A girl who worked in a nearby restaurant. Scratch? American Bar and Grill? Her sprayed hair still racked up in a tease, her eyeliner smudged, her mouth open in much the same vapid, sad smile she had when she was awake.

On a low teakwood table, a small hand mirror with "Hollywood, Here I come!" stenciled on it, and a razor, and a couple of rolled hundred-dollar bills. (He gave them to the girls afterwards; their thrills, then, were doubled.) He looked down at his body. Still firm, muscular, tan. The girl, twenty years younger than he, was the one who had aged. Lines by her mouth, lines around her eyes; little, white, round, soft, cantaloupe belly.

He reached under a flowered bolster, part of this whole futon thing, found Lorna's tour itinerary. "Whatever you do, I'll know it," she'd told him as she'd flown off for a six-week tour to make thousands of dollars on the lecture circuit and turn the rest of the country on to her particular brand of carefree Christianity. "I'll know it and I won't care, because I'll be coming back."

He'd worked so long and hard to be cool, developed such a shell, that he'd been able to smile and yet be negligent, move his beautiful hands in her shining hair, feel his prick move as she waved her hands at it, saying, "See? I can keep you hard for hours, *days* if need be . . ." And he saying, "Don't take all the credit" or, "Don't press your luck" but then surrendering to it—just as she advised on television. And truly, for hours at a time, he was able to work miracles, more than with anybody else ever before.

Before she'd left she'd given him permission: "Have your little girls, the way you always do," she'd said. "I'm not in the business of denying you pleasure. I'm in the falling-in-love business."

"I've finally met my match," he said courteously. "At last I've met my equal." Then as she gazed at him, "Someone my own age at least," and she threw back her head and laughed.

But there was someone else his own age, someone he called every day at three-thirty in the afternoon, someone he took to premieres or any charity fund-raiser having to do with Democrats, animals, or the sick. His wife: chaste as Calpurnia, and as tedious.

And it was she to whom his thoughts returned this morning, even as he checked that Lorna (staying this week at the Helmsley Palace) would get her two dozen white roses every day.

He got up. Pulled on some chinos. Walked across the long expanse of polished floor to where a corner of the

vast room screened off a tiny kitchen. One of his secretaries had already been here, made coffee, squeezed orange juice, put two almond croissants in the microwave.
Left out the *Times*, open to the "Calendar" section. But
he looked at page one of the real part of the paper, reg-
istered the headline. Walked again, holding his coffee, past
the covered, sunken, silent, hot tub, past the word processor, past the stereo equipment—mechanical ghosts in
the coiling wisps of fog—out onto the small balcony, one
of three or four that opened off the second floor, and
looked out onto the strand.

He saw, on the beach, in the very early morning,
benches already filled with old women, a couple of tall
black men repeating last night's coupling in a urine-stained
doorway. He saw street merchants opening their vans, setting out T-shirts on strings in the fog, the sound of the
dead ocean far out, slapping against fouled grey sand.
What he saw must have made up his mind for him.

Or maybe it was the headline for that day, who knows?
People got scared in increments. L.A. PREPARES FOR
THE UNTHINKABLE could blare at you for days and
weeks, and then just one thing, one run-over dog could
turn you on to it.

Maybe it was the soft girl in his bed with her smeared
makeup. Maybe it was her terror, or her decay. We do
know he did it that one last time, because she became a
folk heroine for a while—the very last chicklet Franz got
it up for.

All we know is, after the breakfast, and a snort, and
one last screw, he said, no, they couldn't go in the tub
again, he had some work. He gave her the rolled hundred,
walked her as far as the top of the stairs, saw her—from
his window—climb into the called cab, and then went
through the place pulling plugs: the phones, all of them,
the answering machines, the word processor, thereby con-
signing all the bookwork of a multimillion-dollar business

to oblivion. He unlocked the doors to his film storeroom, he unlocked files; there were no secrets to keep anymore. He finished the last of his coffee, walked down the stairs to where his two secretaries were already at work, told them to call him a cab too. They, concealing their surprise, did so, and when the second lonely checkered little sucker finally found its way through the shrouded streets where his studio maintained its unmarked, unsigned location, Franz dropped one set of car keys on one girl's desk and the other set on the other girl's desk and moseyed out into the mist without saying goodbye.

It wasn't until later in the day, when one of their girlfriends who worked at Vicente Foods or Westward Ho called up to say Callie deGeld had ordered food up to the Brentwood house for three months, including fifty cases of Dom Perignon, and what the hell was going on? that they had the wit to go upstairs and discover the thawing ice, the disconnected phones, the disappeared accounts, and, underneath the handmade cedar planking that kept his hot tub free of household dust, the script he'd been developing for the past six months—a simple love story—drowned.

Lorna wouldn't find out about it for sure for another five days, when she moved to Boston, to the Ritz Carlton, and the roses stopped coming.

THIS IS THE WAY THE DARK AGES LOOKED. IT WAS HOT, and it stank. It wasn't exactly like in the movies, but it was grey and dark and smoky. You tasted the thick air. I'm talking of the years right after. People wore blankets for a long time. I think they wore blankets because the working people had memories of polyester burns, their clothes melting into their skin, or watching that happen to others. Because of the feeling of clothes on raw skin, on sores—if you could find any loose cloth, if there was any—that was the best thing to wear.

Plants grew back right away, with the first rains. It was dangerous to drink the water. It was hard to know where you were, since there were vast craters and mountains where before there had been none. When a person's skin burned away, it grew back as cracked brown hide. We became experts on the wind. The prevailing westerlies were the ones to go out in; the Santa Anas coming down from the northeast—that in the old days used to scour the city's air—were the ones now to make you take shelter. Even today, when the air darkens and the taste gets thick on the tongue, our people—without saying much—take shelter.

There was little crime. At first there was panic, looting, suffering, fire. The panic—many who live remember it. It seems funny now. People fell where they were in the streets. They prayed on their knees, they wept. (On the other hand, some didn't.) In the last minutes, women turned on their husbands: *"You, you did this!"* speaking in tones, the tones they had used before only when giving birth, so that some men, even in the midst of their great fear were blown off the planet looking sheepish. By *you*, the women meant men, males: Caspar Weinberger, Alexander Haig, Ronald Reagan, but afterwards they couldn't remember those names, only the shape of the missiles and the bragging and bullying that had preceded these times. For a while a few women went to the few intact male corpses they could find, castrated them, pinned the bloody, dried penises to walls and tree trunks, with the scrawled word *peacekeeper*, but soon it didn't seem worth the trouble. Blacks halfheartedly offed whites; and whites settled scores, but it wasn't worth the trouble; panic prevailed.

We hear that people gathered material wealth but didn't know what to gather. The price of oil in El Segundo had gone up at the very first; but then cars became useless except as dwellings and armor. Anything that plugged in was useless, but the wiring was valuable. Canned food, first thought to be valuable, often had turned into deadliest poisons. People collected things, made caves, tried to find buildings, but it was chancy.

Then fires swept through, worse than the bombs, because there was no warning, no help for them; no reason and no "cause." There was no *you* to blame but the fires. You chose to stand or run. This is when people believed that the end of the world had really come, because that's what it looked like, that's what it sounded like—the terrible roar, the walls of flames. People stood rather than knelt and cried, Jesus, Jesus! as they prepared to burn. Sometimes, arms outstretched, they ran straight in.

I'm getting ahead of myself. That's also an effect of what happened. Time changed; you never knew what day it was anymore, you couldn't remember how long ago it had started to happen, or how long it took when it did happen. (Some of the dates, even the years, I put down in this story may be wrong.) But listen to me. Some people say it was a bad time, but I say it was a good time.

THERE WERE THE LAST FEW WEEKS "IN FRONT." WE ALL watched TV (TV, how strange!). All those men had their last chance to be important, and you can't say they didn't give it their best shot. Those were the days of the two-thousand-dollar business suits, when everybody who had an opinion about anything got interviewed, and then loyal wives got cricks in their necks from looking up at them, but every once in a while, if you could tear your eyes away from whoever was talking about the grave danger we were in, you saw—sometimes—the wives falter, bring their eyes down, look into the middle distance, shudder, shiver.

Those were the days of terror, but they were short days, fourteen to forty as I remember, when we either broke away or stayed. Every day, in eight- and ten-hour special "reports" the screen showed us the riots at L.A. airport as would-be passengers brought down their wealth—their jewels, money, wristwatches, heroin and cocaine, and waved them at harried personnel behind counters, whose computers were *already* blowing up and out. Or the stupid ones, the really stupid ones, who lived in the goatish eastern suburbs of L.A.—Pomona, Covina, Alhambra, Upland—took their impulse to flee but took it *east.* Can you believe it? Besieging the rich at Palm Springs, hiking or driving with great anguish up and over the Cajon Pass, with apparently not the slightest knowledge that what they would find on the other side of the mountains was miles of desert waste, and prime military targets as well. Of course the Air Force rose to the moment and defended that desert, making occasional strafing runs just to take out a few cars and terror-stricken civilians; saying to anyone who held a microphone in front of them that these grinding General Motors vehicles, loaded to the gills with grandmothers and mattresses and Cuisinarts and sobbing shit-stained babies, were subversives, hotfooting it over the pass to prevent the imminent launching of our weapons.

Well, it was ugly to watch, but the general feeling, even then, was those people were so dumb they didn't deserve to live. And we felt the same way about the rictus-grinning housewives who bought out the stores and got themselves photographed in supermarkets, as though buying three cases of chocolate pudding powder was going to save them.

We watched all that on television with disgust and dread and very strong sick feelings, but I'd be lying if I said that when it started we didn't watch it with awe. Excitement. Anticipation. A general feeling of *Wow, I'm ready and here it comes!* For one thing, if you lived in California, what was the Big Deal! Imagine the white-knuckle rides at Magic Mountain, the Simi Valley earthquake (and the floods that came later), and two or three Bel Air fires whooshing up at once; that was what it was like, and finally, of course, the relieved sense that *it was* going to happen; and we wouldn't have to spend any more time worrying about *whether* it was going to happen.

As I say, I lose chronology here, but I also say it's a miracle that I can remember the *word* chronology. The way I remember, we couldn't think of what to do. Everyone fell back on what they used to do anyway.

Thus, the housewives in the supermarkets, the frantic drivers with their frightened families stranded in the Cajon Pass or way out in the wastes of the high desert on the Palmdale Road. Please don't think I'm putting on the dog when I say that *our* friends, *our* family, spent that last couple of weeks making long-distance phone calls and making love.

And there were those of us who spent the "last" two or three weeks at La Toque, or Michael's, or the American Bar and *Grill—that* got a few laughs—or Spago or the Polo Lounge. Or we said farewell at last long elegies at tiny Mexican joints on the west side where the *mariachi UCLAtlan* sang until their voices cracked, and Mexican wives who'd spent their lives not saying or doing or (supposedly) thinking anything, finally stood up, and with tears streaking their faces, sang *La Llorona* or *Cama de Piedra* but mostly the joyous songs, and whole restaurants—I'm speaking now of the Mexican ones—would be given over to singing and dancing and drinking tequila with lemon wedges until dawn, and usually after.

Do you see why I say that even *then*, even those two or three weeks *before*, could have been a good time, depending on how you looked at it?

Over at Michael's—because there were so many who wanted a "last meal" there—they pushed the tables together and let people eat family-style. Florists all over the city had "folded their tents" and let their roses wither, so the handsome waiters at Michael's scurried out and plundered all the gardens of Santa Monica to bring back great branches of bougainvillea and entire plants of furiously blooming marguerites. And let us all remember this! Michael himself, who through the years had taken such fierce pride in owning the very finest place in town, made a last bid for the divine, for historical immortality. He laced his delicate sauces in those last days with enough old-fashioned LSD that the flowers, the trees in that garlanded patio, the desserts, began to *breathe* in that sweet way most of us hadn't seen since the sixties, and you saw, instead of bodies around you, a couple of hundred souls at the tables. During those interminable last feasts, you might look across at—well, there was the lady from the second *Invasion of the Body Snatchers* who'd gained a little weight, but it didn't matter *now*, and upon request she'd make her eyes dance for the people around her. And tears were shed at that exquisite sight.

While nine-tenths—my guess—of the city of eleven million were *leaving*, driving over that Cajon Pass to the Mojave Desert, or sneaking (oh, irony!) across the border into most unwelcoming Mexico, or driving hopefully to a midpoint between here and San Francisco, or commandeering boats in the marina to float as far out into the ocean as possible, or taking matters into their own hands with bullets, or the box of pills, or the last and final family fight— a tenth of us were staying.

This is what you often saw. Since you knew that every ride in a car was apt to be your last, and since that Pope Whatever-His-Name-Was had got such good press by kissing the ground of whatever country he touched down in, you saw—well, you would have seen all of us touching our cheeks and noses to the ground when we got out of cars. Or when we approached our still-intact homes. You saw little wives in front yards with their arms *embossing* tenderness, kissing the sides of their houses, for instance, or burying their faces in their children or their pets. I saw one older lady flat on her back on her front lawn looking up into a bed of birds-of-paradise.

Oh, Paradise! This is what we found.

Every minute was your minute to make a choice: It was turn on the television and watch some hated white man tell you about hell, or it was lie down on damp green grass—or the dry weeds of Topanga, or the red ants of Lancaster—and say thank you, I love you, I love this.

And as I said before, you can imagine the sack time we put in! It wasn't desperate time, or brutal. It wasn't what came afterward when it was catch-as-catch-can for a few years.

The morning after Aurora left, Skip and I drove down for a lunch at Michael's. When we began to go back up the coast, we stayed on top of the palisades—those lovely cliffs—instead of hitting the highway by the beach. We passed Felicia's luxury apartment, and—pointing it out to Skip—I saw Hal there on the balcony, beaming with joy, waving with one arm at us, hugging someone with the other. It was his own Felicia, come home to be with him.

There were other places, easy to rent now, along that short drive, and we took one for the afternoon. Would we stay here until the very end? Or would we go home? As long as Denise knew where we were, it didn't matter. We trusted the universe to let us all be together.

Never have I felt such tenderness for any man as for my own dear Skip when we lay down in some retirement hotel on the Santa Monica bluffs. Still, when you went out on your terrace, there were senior citizens taking the last clean air. They waved at us and laughed as we kissed, and I clenched my fist in a revolutionary salute.

Then we were lying side by side, looking out onto another delicious set of swaying palm fronds, the giddy ocean behind them, and *wow*, what can I *say*? We learned once and forever what it was to have the world fall away, to be

one soul, to forget, to shiver and weep with happiness, to
look into each other's eyes until you couldn't look anymore, because our tears came and our fingers trembled. It
was love without children or future or past, not even
"love" the way you'd been brought up to think of it, but
just a bright pink light around our heads like those silly
halos in holy cards, and you knew you were getting ready
for eternity—no doubt about it now.

And there were mercy fucks and revenge fucks, and I
can't die without fucking her/him fucks, but you have those
everywhere and every time, even now, I'm sorry to say.

WHEN LORNA RETURNED FROM HER TOUR IT WAS TIME
for her to give her "You Can Master Fear by Going Straight
Into It" talk, and she gave that one six or eight times a
day—not just on TV but all around the west side for, we'll
say, twenty-one days. So what would that be, maybe a
hundred and fifty times? But as you might imagine there
were end-of-the-world-maniacs on every corner saying, I'm
not even kidding, *Repent! Repent!* And people down on
their knees saying, as if it would make a difference, "We
do! Oh, Jesus, we do!" and Lorna wasn't popular in those
last days, not nearly as popular as she might have wished.

"I am a girl from Los Angeles State College," she
would begin, telling her story. "And I got my education
in a quonset hut." Her dyed, curly, sun red hair hung
down in flat sheets. She spoke in the homes of Jane Fonda
and Norman Lear, though neither of them was present at
the time. She spoke at the Amfac Hotel, a stone's throw
from the airport, because she was trying desperately to
leave America in those last days. She spoke wherever people asked her to, and as she spoke the sweat poured off
her face and, as often as not, the tears streamed down.
But, then, that was normal.

I tried to hear her at least once a day. I see now I was

asking too much of her—to take away my fear, or soften it, or dent it—*are you kidding*? But it gave some of us the gist of a Christianity we could understand; that poor guy up on the cross, and before that happened to him, *he* was so scared, his face came off on a towel.

The end of our world was at hand, and nothing she or anybody else could say could change it. But, conversely, the fires hadn't started yet; there was nothing to get excited about. There was just the perfectly trimmed corner yard of Franz deGeld's exquisite Brentwood home, and him most probably locked up inside with his wife, his children, his hardwood floors.

Lorna stayed away from Franz's house itself; but she did come six or seven times to his quiet green lawn hidden by hedges to preach, and—as usual—mostly women came to hear her. The women dressed up, in everything but stockings. They were on their way to make love, or eat, or make peace with their parents or their children, and they listened with a horrible desolation and resignation, because the truth is that during that time the light sometimes left Lorna; don't ask me how, or why. Her message was about fear.

"I came from L.A. State College, do you know where that is? And I got my education in a quonset hut. My subject today is fear, and that you can go beyond that fear, on the other side of fear, by allowing yourself to go into it, experience it. Take, for example, my own fear of public speaking . . ."

But, of course, by that time, we weren't thinking of our fear of public speaking.

"I have always had the experience of coming close to success, to what I wanted, and then, as often as not, it would fall through. I have studied kinesiology; I know that very often even our muscles conspire against us. Haven't you ever stood—as I'm doing now—up in front of people and the muscles that move your tongue refuse to move, your knees shake and buckle, even as mine are doing now? I've found that if you don't express fear, it does not go away. It lodges somewhere in your body. It goes out through your arms as violence . . .''

Standing in the crowd, because she would be forever my friend, I'd try to go along with her, thinking back on all of the short history of the United States that I could remember, wondering, why didn't John Foster Dulles, why didn't that MacNamara, why didn't that Caspar, why didn't they all just let their fear stay *fear*, for God's sake?

But, of course, standing there on the grass in the hot sun, trying, trying for a grip on religion, or at least history, it was difficult. I kept thinking about the cheese enchiladas at the Hacienda, or the fresh swordfish in ginger sauce at Michael's; thought about the spirit of my father (where Carlos Casteneda had always said it should be, behind my left shoulder) where death was. *Dad*? It seemed like he might be smiling, but I couldn't be sure.

Lorna worked Brentwood, Santa Monica, Malibu. We usually found her every day, maybe twenty or fifty of us, at about ten-thirty in the morning. We dressed in summer clothes, some of us in hats.

''Fear will most often come out in violence, but sometimes it manifests in paralysis. You can *see* what you want, but you're unable to reach out your arms to *own* what is yours, to *decree* what is yours! *Because you deserve the very best, and now is the time for it*! There are miracles, there are miracles for all of us now, even now, if we have the strength to reach out . . .''

She hadn't been eating, and her always wiry little body was shrunken now. Her silk blouses darkened and clung to her breasts, drenched with sweat. ''We are in Heaven even as I speak. Believe me. That's not to say there isn't such a thing as fear. Listen. Once there was a seminar I was supposed to address. I'd never done it before. Was I

frightened? You'd better believe it! I was frightened until
the world looked level . . ."

"Lorna?" a voice quavered; a woman in her early forties. Tall but no more than a hundred and ten pounds. I
knew from our few words together in these mornings that
she spent these last days in *dance* classes, eight or ten
hours a day, perfecting, I can only suppose, her perfect
body in God's eyes. "Lorna, will you teach us how to
pray?"

Will you believe me that the *burning* started then and
there? Lorna wore plain white, medium-heel pumps.
Where our heels sunk into the damp green grass of Franz
deGeld's estate (if we were imprudent enough to wear
them), her heels floated on the surface, as if that spongy
turf were green concrete. I was staring at those immacu-
late, perfect pumps, because I couldn't bear to look at
Lorna's face, and from out of Lorna's heels I saw—I didn't
see fire, but I saw the grass parch up and shrivel in con-
centric circles for not far, three or four inches only.

"I can't," she cried. "You know all that better than I
do. There is no *asking* for anything! There is no *getting*
anything. We have it *now*. We either have it now or we
don't!"

A few women started crying, a few men walked away.
I don't know if Lorna said it or I thought it, and it doesn't
matter. What had "Our Father" done for us? Who was
there to pray to now but Kali, Goddess of Creation and
Destruction? And what in the hell were we going to say
to some Indian grudge-holding looney-tune lady goddess
with twenty arms or so? What would we ask for? To survive? To die? To be saved? Saved from what? *For* what?

"We either live in Heaven or we don't live," Lorna
said, and tears streaked her face. "You dumb bunnies, I
don't know anymore than that and neither does anybody
else."

She looked often, during these morning talks, toward

the windows in Franz deGeld's mansion. Sometimes I'd
follow her glance, sometimes a curtain would move, but
during the last days there seemed to be nobody home. As
I say, there was adequate time—*did* I say that?—for the
agile, the determined, to get out. To leave the country, or
the planet if they wished. And every minute you stayed
inside your country, or your house, or your body, you were
making the choice.

WHY I DIDN'T LEAVE? TO BE PERFECTLY FRANK, I NEVER
thought I'd be the one to stay. I never bought my children
earrings but I didn't think, "They'll be able to take these
out of the country when the time comes." On the other
hand, I never drove a canyon but I didn't think of its high
earth walls as shelter, and I never was so disgusted with
a string of pearls as when I learned that pearls cannot
survive flames, that they melt and puff into an ugly mess,
and lose their value.

It turned out I couldn't leave, didn't want to leave, because of my family, and my friends, and who I was. Skip,
in his courage, had shamed me.

Persistence. Surrender. Lorna's words. And if I use her
words, it's because I didn't like the others. Persistence.
You could get out, if you really wanted to. For the others,
ice cream until the end. Surrender. I must admit I'd never
known what she meant by "surrender" until those last days
before the end and the beginning. All it *meant* was surrender. One afternoon or midday, Skip moved from our
bed onto the balcony to look, to look. And on the next
balcony, another couple. All we could do was weep and
grin. We reached out our arms across that small space—
our fingers touched.

Why I didn't leave was food and love and sex and palm
fronds, but let's get serious. As the sun broke through the
late part of the day, it was time for us to go home, to our

"real life." (And there were those who went to work until
the end, fought the thinning rush hour until the end.) As
the sun hit four o'clock, everyone in the city went home
to their families. And it was then that I learned (twenty-
five years after I'd heard about it in some class) about the
Great Chain of Being. My father was on my left shoulder,
but my mother was still in this life and had come down
from her home in the desert to be in our house, where she
spent those last days of the cusp in our garden. Aurora
was safe and gone. She would live and remember. Denise
stayed here, with four or five friends; they moved each
night from one home to the next.

Finally, it was the city that held us, the city they said
had no center, that all of us had come to from all over
America because this was the place to find dreams and
pleasure and love. I noticed—looking at headlines—that
some cities emptied and some didn't. Ours didn't, not
completely. It may be argued, of course, that the hundreds
of miles of desert that surrounded us had something to do
with it, but I don't think so. (And if there was any rage I
felt, outside of the terror that periodically seized up my
body like a Porsche engine running without oil, it was a
fury that "they" were finally going to have the nerve to
take our defenseless little adobe houses and turn them back
to blowing dust.) They said we were crazy to stay. But
then someone had always said we were crazy to be here
in the first place. And someone had always said Noah was
crazy to build a boat in his desert, and Lot had been crazy
to pack up, on an impulse, and head west.

So when it came to leaving, I found I couldn't. I couldn't
even take off my pearls. They were just going to have to
melt around my neck. I had to apologize in my mind for
all those things I'd ever thought about the Jews. Why didn't
they get out of Germany!? Because they didn't want to?
Because they decided the only thing to do was "experience their fear and go through it"?

At home we played Scrabble. We stocked up on dry goods, inefficiently. We cleaned the house. We had people over for dinner. We bought the book of truly tasteless jokes and laughed our brains out. Why do girls have two holes? So you can carry them like bowling balls, wasn't that it? We all slept in the same room together; my mother and I and Skip in one bed; Denise and her friends—when they were at our house—in and around another double bed we'd pulled into the big bedroom.

And, sure, every day each of us would bring something more home; a hundred dollars' worth of Lindberg Varsity Pack vitamins, a sack of rice, some earthenware crocks for water, or raisins, or those pills that were supposed to protect your thyroid from radiation.

ONE MORNING IN THE FIRST PART OF JULY, WE DECIDED not to drive down to the beach. It was a national holiday, there were supposed to be fireworks set off by the pier. It wasn't the kind of thing we wanted to see. Denise and her friends had spent the night, and a new neighbor from next door was outside busily mowing his weeds with a power-scythe. My mother wanted us to dig up a patch so she could plant some root vegetables for all. It was an ugly day, muggy and overcast; no one wanted to go anywhere anyway. When we woke up late, it was like a not-very-fun slumber party, with that crowded room on a hot, muggy summer morning, and all those kids we hardly knew. Skip got up and made us all coffee. Our last.

When it came, all we felt was a tilt in the earth, and the sky lit up but not very brightly. Then, in less than two minutes, the window jolted and fell from its casing into the room. It didn't even break. We felt the rush of thick air, and put our heads under the sheets. Skip turned on the transistor radio, but my mother said "*No!* Turn it off.

What we don't know won't hurt us." And the air began to burn.

Denise, whose grammar school teacher had been predicting the end of the world since before she'd even started kindergarten, observed morosely, "This is going to make Mr. Russo very happy." Then, in the way that fatigue overwhelms you when the brush fire threatens, all eight of us dropped into sleep as if we'd been felled, as if life had served us a collective mickey finn.

The real fire came the next day. We had been ready for it for weeks; our trash cans filled with water at each corner of the house, our rags damp. Four of us stood on the roof tamping out sparks, one at each corner while the others handed up water. The fire roared down at us like a train.

And it passed us by. Our house survived. The rest of the world was ashes.

Now is where the bad part comes; I don't know how much I should tell you. How much do *you* remember? I know that whatever I'd learned of fear up until that time was only joking, a masquerade of fear. There was no question, after that, of bravery or nobility or doing the right thing, or even *fear*. Or even day or night.

Our skin had seared, and since we had wrapped up in almost everything we had to fight the fire, most of our skin sloughed off in our jackets, in our jeans and boots. We crept back to our upstairs room, knowing we should be in basements, garages, holes in the ground, but trusting the great earthen walls of the canyon to protect us. In our agony we needed beds, and to lie down, and be with each other.

Water was all we thought about. And the dying squirrels that ran squeaking in the fine ash of the canyon, leaving trails like tiny toboggan slides. You'd see them later, dead, their little paws turned up. We became fanatics about our arms, having read somewhere that you would die right away if your skin, once pinched, stayed pinched. So if some one of us was crying, we'd grab an arm—they'd grab mine, I was a great crier in those days—and say *hang on, hang on*, it won't be today! Day after day went by, and it wasn't.

If there were histories now, they'd say that plague killed the city, and thirst. But it was mostly fear that killed. Fear was the killer in those first few months. There weren't words to use for it. Remember, our house was on the crescent of a hill, in a canyon north of the city and east of the beach, and we'd go out each day, one at a time, and walk that two-hundred-foot crescent, to be sure we could still walk, to see if things had changed. We'd come upon piles of vomit, as we walked. That was the other reason we walked, to go outside and vomit. We felt that what we vomited was the "sick," part, and that what was left upon our bones would grow back healthy. When I went to walk one day, out at the far edge of the point, I saw a kid, one of ours, writhing.

He turned to look at me—I saw it was a "he," not my own beloved daughter—and I saw that his neck was swollen like a fullback's, he was black, black as a Bic, black as tar, black as coal, black as the Pit. *So, so, this is it*, is what I thought.

"Can I bring you anything?" I asked, but he looked out of his eyes with detachment, and I believe he was thinking *this is it* as well, with a sort of relief built in. And another boy went out soon after.

We let them stay there and for a week or so took our walks in another direction. When any of us felt the beginning of a stiff neck, we dosed ourselves with penicillin. When my mother died some weeks later, it could have been from a natural death. We took her out on the point; she shriveled to nothing in the sun. We found, in fact, that the dry climate of L.A. lent itself to this ancient way of

taking away the dead: let them lie there and dry seemed
to be what people said later that they had done. Don't go
near a tainted body, don't taint the soil by putting them
underneath it. And we heard about terrible suffering later,
but no more, actually less, than we had thought of it before.

The deaths by thirst we heard of later were the worst,
and the discomfort from thirst was the worst. Where we
lived, in the ashen, chilly canyon, there was a creek perhaps a mile away, and when the sky was cold and grey
but the air was quiet enough to see through the swirling
clouds of ash, two of us would take our turn to creep down
to the creek or to the spring above it and bring home two
pans of water. Rice would go into one pan to soak soft,
and the other we would divide to sip and drink. If we
vomited, we gave what was left of our water to the others.

After a few weeks, I think there were still six of us:
Skip, my daughter, two of her friends, and our neighbor,
Richard, who had lived a hundred yards up from us in the
canyon. He was an extremely neat man and busied himself
when he went outside, raking the ashes away from the
house. "This is still a home," he would say when I'd give
him a look. "We must keep it as nice as we can." Five
out of eleven dead, was that it? And all around us, no sign
of life. For weeks and days we didn't "explore"; no one
wanted to find anything. Our food supply stayed fairly
even. We were very sick, of course.

Was there a miracle in this? How could we know if there
was or not? Was it the miracle of the loaves and fishes—
one of Lorna's very favorite stories—that two thirty-pound
sacks of brown rice lasted us until the first rains came?
Every morning when we woke, the six of us (I think), in
two wide double beds pushed together, the dark grey stiff-
ened sheets alive with fleas, our nightgowns covering
sores and scabs, one of us would be sure to reach, cursing,
into his mouth to pluck out a tooth and then carefully

swallow the blood that came from that soft red hole. It's true that first, as we woke, transfixed with terror and then relief, we sat up, one by one, and touched each other to be sure we were not dead. We plucked our forearms and each other's forearms tenderly, and sometimes with an extra little pinch. Sometimes one of us might stand up and move over to the glass we had stuck back up in that upstairs bedroom window, look at the swirling ash that had persisted for weeks, darkening everything to night when the slightest breeze came up, and croak out, in the choked voices we spoke with then, "OOOO-eee! I see abundance *everywhere*!"

The neighbor, who still slept by himself, curled in a corner, looked on impassively as we . . . I supposed you'd have to say, we laughed.

Was it a miracle, then, that when the rains came and it was necessary to let the water stand for at least a week before we could drink it—and was that when we lost two of my daughter's friends whose names I forget?—that slogging out one morning we saw clustered (under the overhanging side of a broken retaining wall we'd built so long ago) maybe fifty snails, and, shivering, soaking wet, bald and raving, my ancient, never-dying, forever chivalric friend said, again, "OOOO-eee! I see abundance *everywhere*!" Then, with the exaggerated panache of a Parisian dandy, he reached over, plucked one away from the crumbling concrete, held it up against the drizzling poisoned rain to wash away the ash, and with a hideous sucking noise that I remember even now, removed it, protesting, from its shell and sent it sliding to its own Armageddon.

"You could get *sick*," I protested, and I saw his stomach heave in protest, but he kept it down and grinned a toothless Richie Havens grin at me, so that—what could I do? Was I less daring? Could I say *no* to fabled "abundance"? I picked one up (remembering how many of those mollusks I'd already consigned to oblivion by standing, in the lost days, on

the crescent rim, lobbing them down, *down* into the dry climate, screeching *"Death to all snails!"*), put it to my lips,
and sucked. It resisted, then slid on my tongue and down my
throat, cool and accommodating. Our first food since the lost
days, except rice, water, Lindberg Varsity Pack vitamins,
and penicillin. What I'm saying is, Would we have seen
abundance in those filthy, unattractive shells had we not been
looking for it?

WE WERE COMPLETELY CUT OFF FROM EVERYONE AND
everything, and that was the way we liked it. My mother, in
her more cantankerous days, had asked us repeatedly to turn
off the hysterical messages on the radio, and one early night
had taken the batteries out and hidden them. "I'll tell you
where they are," she said, affecting senility, "some day. *If*
you're good." But she passed on before she told us, and we
hadn't gone over her body for them as we carried her out to
the point.

From time to time now, when we went to the bottom of
the canyon to get water, we'd see others, but they looked
unreal and comical, stooped over and wearing grey rags,
with no hair and no teeth; some of them plainly dying and
all that. But I suppose that none of that seemed *real* to us.
Physical suffering, if it belongs to someone else, can be easily borne.

This is how it would be.

After we woke up in the morning—not really morning
that we could actually tell in those early days because, as
I say, grey ash shadowed all—we would go outside and
shit. Then come in and, with our right hands, scoop up a
handful of soaked rice from a pot and let it lie in our
mouths to suck. We had sores and holes in our mouths
and the rice was soothing. It was amazing, it took an
eternity, an *endless* time, to eat that softened grain. One
or two of us would take an hour to pace the crescent of

the hill, not keeping watch, just looking around, holding umbrellas to keep off bad air. Then two of us would begin to walk in the other direction down to the canyon floor with two dented pans, going to get water. We walked with cloth tied over our noses and mouths. To breathe in the ash was frightening and most unpleasant. It might take the better part of a day to get down to the creek and back. We'd walk without talking. I can't speak for the others, but I never thought much. When I did, it seemed the thought was absolutely new.

As when, down at the creek, on the other side there might be three women, shrouded, dipping in with pans, hunched and filthy, and you might think, Ingmar Bergman movie! And then you'd think, no more Ingmar Bergman, no more movies! But no one scurried away, and no one was afraid to send the girls down alone, because the very idea of lifting a hand against another person for any reason was absolutely out of the question.

We didn't wave at each other or say, "Are you doing OK?" We did notice the scabs and sores, and hoped they weren't too sick, but it was as though there was all the time in the world to talk. There was all the absolute time in the world. Walking home, holding the water carefully, one of us might whisper, "Ingmar Bergman." And the other one might smile.

The only time I can remember terror down on Old Topanga Canyon Road was when, as several of us were silently dunking our pans into the shallow stream (and it took all the time in the world to do it right, to hold the pan so that the clearest liquid might seep over the lid of the pan, to avoid the sometimes very hideous things that oozed on the bottom, to avoid the pale foam that collected at the side), a noise, I can't even tell you what a noise, a hideous, barking metallic vibration shook us all. Another weapon! And just as the aftershocks of an earthquake are far more frightening than the first jolt, I saw stark terror, heard yowls and whimpers from them all and from myself, and from out of a bank of ashes, faster than a snake platoon, a figure flashed past us and *out of sight*, leaving an odor of shit and fear, and the shit was right there in spots on the pitted road.

"He tried to . . ." I couldn't think what it was he'd tried to do.

"He tried to . . ."

We thought about it. And a woman said, "Start . . . start the car?"

We talked about that at home, when we talked, for days.

No, I can't remember when our new ideas all started. And I thought so much about going to Australia in those last days before the war that I can't remember what months up here are supposed to be cold. Because even though they'd said it would be cold, I know it was a long time before things were actually cold again. But things worked out for us more exquisitely than we ever planned! Because when most people were dying, the weather was very dry. Because in our canyon we already knew how to fight the fire. Because whatever had happened all over the world, the snails loved it where we were, and we loved those snails! And by the time the rain had been around long enough for green things to come up, we'd gotten around to thinking of ourselves as alive, *alive!*

Because the green things made us sick as hell, and if we'd gotten that sick in the very first days we'd all have died of pure fright.

We couldn't seem to make the green stuff turn into ourselves. We'd bite down on those clear green threads that came out of the dark, wet, ashy earth, and we'd be crying, because just to say, to think, *green*, made our throats close with sadness. We'd put those green threads in our mouths, where they'd sting our raw cheeks and gums and cut across our tongues like saws or knives. We'd hold them in our mouths, until we couldn't bear it anymore, and swallow, and vomit for hours, long after the green stuff was gone.

Or walking, you'd see one of us squatting on the crescent with his butt over the side, shitting the way we'd been doing it for months, and his head would be down between his knees and with his left hand he'd be plucking grass out of his asshole, threads just as fresh and green and painful on the edges as when they went in.

But we knew we needed the green stuff. And we kept on with the exercise. And you know how sometimes we used to wonder if Lorna was right, when she said *expect a miracle*? She used to talk about Gandhi, who looked a lot like the way we did now, and she said he used to get his nourishment out of the air, by breathing. I think, because we *knew* about it, that we did some of that. We would lay a leaf across our tongues and play at it all day. We would look for a seed, and look at it a long time, and if it didn't look back at us, we'd put it in our mouths. The snails lived for a long time around our house. We did too.

I should say that we never "built" a fire up there in the canyon. We never made one, or wanted one, because the fire that had come by gave us our fill of fire for a long time, and later there were days when people from down in the valley made the long walk up to the top of the canyon trying to get to the beach, and some of them still had burns that, well, I don't want to say anything about it.

To me the thing that seemed most clear and came in clearer every day was that—well, you know! This story proves it. We were *alive*, and going to be alive, and if we were, there were others, we saw them every day. Some noises were coming back. Some birds. Some lizards. The sound of rain, and mud moving. The complaints: coughing, groaning, crying in the night. The neighbor in the corner of our room saying, "Ah, shut up."

* * *

I'M SURE YOU KNOW IT TOOK MOST OF THAT FIRST BLACK summer, the rainy fall and winter, the sickness of the first green spring, and the next summer—where we saw quite a few more plague-dead—and then a rain and then another whole journey of the earth around the sun before we began to think about what we were going to do. (Or maybe I'm wrong about that; it seems too long a time.) But I know that it was green when we began to think. This is not to say that we hadn't done some of that before, but walking now, on the road home from the creek, sometimes we'd wave and say, "How's your *IQ*?" Or I heard my daughter say when she cut herself, "Red, red, the color's dead." Or my friend Skip went out one day in *the . . . brush*! In the *brush*, that's what I mean, the words came back, with the world, and Skip came back with a handful of what looked like black sand.

"Chia seeds," he said, "maybe." He pulled at his mouth with his fingers to show me, and under his tongue, and packed into his cheek was a black wad. "Makes you feel . . ." He made his arms flail, palms up. "You know . . . lots of energy!"

My skin, by now, was halfway healed, but it itched. You know how those days were, there was nothing to do, so one afternoon I took out my old leather briefcase and opened it up. The rocks looked as good as they always had. I picked up a ruby and put it in my mouth. It hurt! Then I held it in my fingers. How red it was! I . . . do you remember how you used to drip hot wax on your arms, or pluck your eyebrows? Or pick a pimple? I took that stone and put it on the back of my left hand, and pushed. Would that stop the itching? The ruby broke through the skin and stayed. It felt like—did you ever have psoriasis and hold your hands under scalding water? It felt awful, and good. From then on, when I had nothing to do, I'd take a stone and wiggle it, teasing my itching, flaking, diseased skin, and stick that stone in there! So that after a few months, my hands were like glittering stone gloves. Very heavy, but they looked good!

One day we took our sheets out in the sun and stamped on them and poured water so they'd smell like . . . see what I mean! *Laundry! Wow*. We began to laugh. Laundry. (Although the dry and crusty sheets hurt our skin for a week after, and we didn't do that for a while again.)

Then we started saying "Hi!" and "Howyadoin!" as we walked down for water. Then we started saying "Howsyrold man!" Then one day one of our girls came home all flowsy and flustered. A man had been following her. OOO-eee.

The great thing is, she couldn't even remember why it was anybody would have been following her! When we told her, she said, *"You're kidding!* He'd really want to do *that?"* And next time she slowed down so he could catch up to her, but he got scared and hid back in the bushes.

Because by then there were bushes.

The first time I saw writing again was a sign I'd seen before up in that canyon—*Ive Seen Fire and Ive Seen Rain*. Yes many times before I'd seen that sign, in the old days, when there would have been a series of bad events, floods and fires, and little animals piled up in long, furry, putrid, wavery lines along the old roads. Someone would write on a plank, sometimes in paint, sometimes in charcoal, *Ive Seen Fire and Ive Seen Rain*. I don't know who wrote up this one, but he put it right by the tree trunk down on what used to be Valley Drive—a riverbed now—the way down to Old Topanga Creek. Was it humor, irony, that made him put that sign—that we used to see on a long, unattractive, arid hill between us and the San Fernando Valley—right in the heart of nowhere where we were now, this dark deep ravine, next to the hollow tree that still bore the traces of an earlier, whitewashed warning: *This place defended by shotgun law?*

People stood and looked at that new sign: *Ive Seen Fire*

and Ive Seen Rain. Could they read it? Were we back to reading? Were they trying to remember the song it came from? Were we back to singing?

My friend Skip, impossibly old now, his dark brown skin translucent over luminous bones, looked up one day as we walked the crescent, holding hands. "There's a bird up there," he said. "A phainopepla. They come from the south." Then tears came out of his eyes.

Let me tell you a little of what grew back. Rye grass first, wouldn't you know it? I know we should have thought of eating it, but what we thought of first was *fire*, and tried, a little each day, to pull it out of the ground. Elderberry bushes, and that first crop of elderberries made us sicker than pigs. (No more pigs!) Something with a red flower we called Indian paintbrush; those yellow daisies with the black center called—weren't they black-eyed susans? I saw a snake one day and it scared the shit out of me. And that's what I mean; that's what it did.

It began to be so much fun to *talk*. "I saw a snake. It scared the shit out of me."

"So I see."

Then it isn't as if we'd laugh. But we'd get these shudders. One day, pulling at the rye grass, trying to get it away from the house, a boy, someone I didn't know, or couldn't remember his name, spoke, after weeks and months of silence. "I've been working like a . . . nigger." Then he stopped, and put up his hand to his bald skull. I could *see* his brain in there, laboring away, harder than his skinny little frame. *Nigger? Digger? Chigger? Pigger? Wigger? Siger? Cigar?*

Once, I burst out singing, "If I had a hammer." I looked around for who said it. It was me. I remembered. I'd gone to junior high school with a big . . . *black woman* who went on to be . . . *famous*. And I knew that in the . . . *garage*, there was a . . . *hammer*.

So one thing I didn't lose was the language. But you

could . . . see? that words would change. Garage. Ingmar Bergman. Chicken salad sandwich. Sometimes, when we got so we could go outside after the sun went down without being afraid, we would do a . . . game? We would do something like a game, where we would say words, to see what they meant. But sometimes it made us cry, so then we would stop. But there was another word, *sad*? When we saw tears, we'd say, *sad*? In the first weeks we'd pinched each other, but that was different, that was medicinal. Now it got so that we could put out our arms, our hands, and put them on the others, the skin of others, and they? him? her? he? she? wouldn't . . . run, or flinch, or shriek? Squeak? Because at night we slept with the long lines of our skins together, motionless, and loved that, but to be poked by a finger, in the day, as we moved, was very hard, like having your *fingernails* pulled out. It brought back those first black weeks. But we didn't have fingernails anymore. Finger . . . *nails?* And we might tap against something, remembering. And little, a little at a time, we might shiver and let ourselves be touched.

HERE'S THE THING ABOUT MEMORY. YEARS, YEARS BEfore, before the end and the beginning, we'd had a dog. Or, was it a coyote? It was . . . wild. We couldn't touch it. But a year or two after she'd come around our house, she'd finally let us touch her. And then she came into the house, if there was a door left open. Then sometimes we'd watch while she came into the living room and put her head on our knees and look into our eyes. And *then* it came to be that she slept all night in the house, and the minute she'd hear a voice, or one of us turning to the other, she'd gallop upstairs to the bedroom and jump on the bed with all four feet. She loved us so much. When we'd first found her wild and starving, we thought of Ishi, that last California Indian, killed with kindness by the university people up north. She was a girl dog (or coyote), and we called her Isha.

One night, then, after we'd started talking again, after the sun went down, before the moon came up, three of us sat out back—we *hunkered* down, is what we did, and out on the point, at the far end of the crescent, we saw . . . a coyote! The first we'd seen since the end and the beginning. My friend Skip said *"Isha."* That was when I felt pain, my head splitting. "My head is splitting," I said, and my eyes melted. The pain was unendurable. "I can't bear it," I said. In one awful moment I saw it all, our *living* room, and pink and yellow lights at night, and our skins pink and white and whole, not *hole*, and so much, wait a minute, so much, wait, wait, so much *love* that a wild thing, starving from the dark, could come inside and put her head on our knees and look at us for the pure pleasure of looking at us, and on the other side of me, there in the dark now, turning her head away, putting her thin, scrabbly little hands up over the holes in her skull where her ears had been was my . . . *daughter*. And I had another one, somewhere on the surface of this planet, but she was gone.

But I saw them, in that other bright world of the past forever hidden from us, on the other *couch*, pushing and jostling each other, and Skip and me wishing they'd stop!

Oh, how could we have ever wished they would stop.

"I can't bear it," I said, and put my whole self down into the dirt, let my eyes cry into the dirt.

There are people who say that a woman with fire red hair who spoke around the city before the end didn't know what she was talking about, but I say she did. I say she was a miracle. Because as I felt the unendurable pain, and I heard my own young one beginning to wail and put her hands up to her head, and my heart split because I couldn't bear it, I heard my old friend Skip say, "My past is now complete. I bless and release it."

Complete! You bet your life! You bet your ass! I thought of those men on the television set. Were they still with us? Had the breasts of their wives withered and fallen away as mine had? Had their bones splintered? Did they live on . . . did they live? Oh. What had they done. Killers. Devils. The Antichrist.

But before I could lose my soul, I heard that good man speak again: "My past is now complete. I bless and release it." I had a *memory* of clean, strong, healthy, happy people writing their sadnesses on pieces of paper, balling them up like . . . *whiffle balls* and throwing them at *Lyin' Boys*, who put on *reflector glasses* and hit at them with a *sequined* baseball bat.

"I can't. I can't. I can't bear it. My babies." But by that time I could hear myself being *corny*. And I knew I had to stop.

"My past is now complete," he said again. "I bless and release it, remember?"

What if we remembered what we wanted, and blessed and released the rest? What if we took those members of the London branch of the Royal Society in the seventeenth century who'd thought they were *on* to something when they took up science, and whiffled them and the next three hundred years, *away* into the smiling universe?

What if we tried to remember John Donne and the Rolling Stones and driving in the car with the radio on, and lying on clean sheets with perfect bodies looking out at palm fronds, and the clean blue of the biggest ocean, what if we only remember *California?* What if we . . . wait, wait, what if we took the cash and let the credit go?

"My past is now complete, I bless and release it. OOOO-eeee! It's good to be alive, and I *am* alive, here in the heart of infinity!"

Was he saying it, or was I? I turned my head. Skip stood up, dancing back and forth on his long legs, his eyes rolled most of the way back in his head, because part of his lids had been burned off long ago. I could hardly hear him, but I knew what he was saying. Well, why shouldn't I? Didn't we have the same story?

Some say Lorna was a quack. Could that have been what they said? But I say she was magic, because I took all of it, the part I couldn't bear, that little lost dog, that running jump of love, my dead souls, *all* souls, and my beloved dearest daughter, wrapped them first in white light, then in pink, and floated them away to be a star.

I kept the words, and the present. The *present,* get it? I got up on my knees and went over to the poor sweet young woman covering her ears against my noise and said to her, the way I'd said to Isha, long ago, long ago, long ago, "Come on. I'm sorry. Just let me. . . . come on. Just . . ."

It was easier with the kid, with . . . Denise. In only a few minutes, I got her to look at me. I put my hands on her arms and my lips on her cheek.

NOW, I'M NOT SAYING IT WAS EASY. NOT LORNA, NOT EVEN Lion, could say that now and get away with it. I'm just saying it was easier than what we (those of us who *had* thought of it) had thought. There were days after that— after several turns of the planet, in the first recognizable spring—when we'd get the idea, and we'd say it as a joke, "So these are the dark ages!" And then we'd laugh. Because though none of *us* looked so hot, the hills had never been so beautiful. The greens and reds and blues and yellows were almost more than your eyes could take.

And, of course, once we started feeling a little better we had bursts of what you'd have to call—although we didn't like the word—strength. There was a day, in the middle of a spring morning, when all of us were outside taking the sun, when we were—*you* know, Denise was biting on her toes, and my friend Skip rubbed the skin off his legs, and the neighbor, Richard, watched some ants. I was doing sit-ups. I planned to be a very old lady, dark brown, the kind you could pluck up off the ground with a thumb and forefinger, a dwarf, an elf. So I was doing sit-ups.

And one of us said, out of that glorious, living silence, where all you heard was the tickle of the ants on the earth and the air as it moved around birds' wings, "Picnic?"

"Oh, yeah!"

"Summertime?"

"Really!"

The neighbor coughed and spit and said, "What a day for the beach!"

I thought my heart might split again and braced for the pain when I saw that the others were, well, they were thinking about it differently.

"Do you . . ."

"The Indians who lived up here," Skip said, "they did it. They used to go down once a year."

If any of us in this canyon knew anything, we knew that the Indians who lived here had been the last word in incompetence. No farming, no tools, no written language, no "kinship system," nothing except waterproof baskets, and that was only because they hadn't got as far as pottery. And all of us had grown up with the story of the California Indians, those dipshit Chumash, who had rowed over to Catalina Island to gather shells and left a woman over there absentmindedly and didn't get back to pick her up for over twenty years.

"To see Catalina again."

And then we all said it, almost together. "On a clear day you can see . . ."

We didn't just *up and go*.

It took days of talking about it, and our first real worries about survival. But we took to mentioning it down at the creek: "Nice day for the beach!"

* * *

OTHERS OF US WILL TELL THAT STORY OF HOW WE CAME
down that fifth year after the world began, how we traveled
the dozen miles, how we met the others who still lived
down in the main part of the canyon, how we camped for
a while where the two creeks met, down by the old post
office, how we found to our amazement and surprise that
a hundred of us still lived, just in the part we were trav-
eling through. We heard hard tales of people in the next
canyon over, too close to the city. We heard nightmare
tales of the valley, where most of our city had lived; death
by thirst and plague. We heard tales of defense by the
canyon people at the eastern summit, wooden lances
against the poor, the sick, who tried to take refuge in the
highlands. But they could have never lived up here,
really—or the ones who *could* were here with us now.

There were six of us, on our trip to the beach. Skip and
Denise and me. Our neighbor, Richard, by now part of
our family. Two of Denise's friends, Fru and—I forget the
other one. We took blankets. We took chia seeds. We took
the last of our rice. I had my jewels in my hands. The six
of us picked our way down the cracked bits of cement, the
driveway, for what we probably knew then was the last
time. We turned and looked at that house, charred wood
bleached out by sun and blast, a castle. But we didn't feel
sad! We went on down into the slit of Old Canyon past
the wide place in the creek where we'd panned water so
many days, and continued, single file, picking our way
along the damp creekside.

I cannot tell you with what tears and smiles we found,
after three miles, among whitened bones and lush rye grass,
a half-destroyed stone building that had been the old Discovery Inn and found a living skeleton—great grandmother, was
it? Of the old Dear family? That woman, Marge, was it?

Burnt almost black, sitting witless and toothless up against a
flat rock outside the slanting building.

"M,m,m, Marge?" said I.

"Fuck," the living carcass said. "Howareya?"

It took us almost a month, from that junction of the old
canyon and the new to make our way the next few miles down
to the beach. It was frightening, and we weren't good with
fear. The old road that cut into the canyon ledge had been
pushed out, either in the blasts or had been scooped down
by the few cave dwellers who had found perfect shelters and
stayed there. They threw rocks at us as we passed, thinking
we were diseased or maybe just plain butt-ugly. But *they*
were the ones who looked strange to us, with their white
skin, their orange puffs of hair, their nervous dancing.

"Just goin' to the beach," we'd say. "Perfect day for
it! Come on along."

But all of us had our own ways, and these people were
scared of the sun. Since we couldn't take the "road," we
went the simple way, right down at the narrow bottom of
the canyon's crack.

My, it was strange down there! Dense and green, with
large, gaudy flowers. We'd look sometimes and say, "Science fiction."

"Really!"

And we had nightmares at night. We were afraid for the
first time in a long time. And we would *say* that! "Oh, I
don't like this! I'm afraid." Steep stone cliffs kept the sun
from us and almost blotted out the sky.

My daughter began again to call me Mom. "Wait up,
Mom!" And I'd feel her fingers curling into the crook of
my arm. We'd walk in step, lock-step; she right behind
me.

I'm not saying we didn't see some awful things. At that
curve just north of the straightaway that went directly up
the middle of the steepest part of the canyon, we came
upon a stack of six or seven cars loaded with passengers,

who (maybe because of the dampness?) hadn't dried the
way they should. You *know* how bad they looked, and how
they smelled. And there was still the fear of the plague.
We stopped for a long time and watched, trying to figure
out how to get around them, wondering what had happened, wondering if this was a sign that we ought to turn
back. (Wondering too what would be going on with the
drinking water downstream.)

Finally Skip said, "We've lived this long, and for a
reason." And Denise said, "This is about where all of
them used to go off the road before, isn't it? Like, where
people used to kill themselves? So maybe it's just that
there isn't anybody anymore to . . . tow them out!"

That made it better, to think that it was just a collection
of car accidents, but it wasn't that, we knew it. This was
where someone had blown the road above us; and these
cars packed with passengers had been trying to get into
the canyon probably, when the road fell out from under
them . . . or maybe not! Because Denise was right. This
was the place of the accidents. The place where, so long
ago, the ones who didn't make the turn at the top of the
straightaway, so plainly marked, were politely committing
suicide when they drove, instead, out into thin air.

To drive! To commit suicide! To get into an . . . accident. You can see that it was an amazing trip for us.

We went on down, climbing in an arc along a rough
and narrow trail, past those cars, those strange dead
beings, and kept at a good pace past where the straightaway turned again into curves. After a day or two, the steep
steep slopes of the canyon softened again and we came out
again into spongy foothills, with soft pink and yellow flowers, and for the first time got the smell of the sea.

We didn't say much. We kept walking, very slowly, the
rest of that afternoon and evening. All of us were remembering. Our neighbor grunted as he moved and kicked
rocks with his huge horny feet; *he* was remembering, but

we'd never know what. He didn't talk much. And I said, as we passed a certain place, "Mark . . . *Mark* somebody died here in a crash."

Denise said, "There was a big accident I saw here once." Skip said, "I was jogging here once when we first lived together and found a workshirt and picked it up. It was from the county jail."

You can see how it was for us. What it was doing to our brains. So that's why we took it easy. There wasn't any hurry.

This is how we slept those last couple of nights. First my friend Skip, his body a clattery, dear thing with lots of right angles, you could almost hear *him* creak against the ground. Then me, right up against him. Then Denise, dear creature. Some girls and women, I regret to say me among them, had lost their breasts in the first year. It was partly the losing of all extra flesh, partly that all soft parts tended to slough off, and partly, I'm sure, another polite way of saying *Fuck it! It was just a hobby!* But Denise, as that first puff of burning air had blown out our windows, put both baby hands over both her soft breasts, so that they remained now, with the sweet imprint of her fingers as white flower petals out from the centers which in better times . . . well. On the other side of Denise, silent and grumpy, turned away from her, making his back a wall for her, the neighbor, Richard. On the other side of him, the two other girls.

Who could be safer than my daughter and me, holding each other through the night? Our skin, so sore and sad for so long, was strong now; we could lie on stones or on burrs and *feel* them but not feel pain. We would lie down one at a time, snuffling and squirming, and maybe talk. Or sometimes issue an order, "I've got to turn over!" But when we slept we slept straight through, getting over fear, because what could happen to us, all together as we were?

So we took it slow, not seeing any more people but

letting the excitement, the anticipation mount up, letting the newer sun come over us, waking up one morning in a wet fog that made us catch our breath. On that morning Denise said, only half joking, "Nuclear fallout?" But Skip said, "Think of all the water this breeze has blown over," and I felt my eyes hurt at the thought of that large and neutral blue.

"Oh, large and neutral blue," I said, and felt Denise glance me out. "Oh holy, rosy *cross,*" she recited smartly, and I shut up.

"Remember," I said, the next morning as we ambled, oh so slowly down these well-remembered curves, past cars covered with morning glory and fragrant anise, "how the traffic some mornings used to back up all the way to here!"

"Goddamn it!" our neighbor said, out of his doltish reverie. "It takes *forever* here! Why don't they fix the signal! There's no excuse for this!" And thinking *that* over, we slowed down. It took us all day to make another quarter of a mile. We could hear the ocean that night, I think. We bit down on creek frogs for dinner and I was the one who said, "That woman, Marina, who lived in Topanga Gulch, a frog *ate* a wire at her place and it went . . ."

"Electrocuted?" Skip asked.

Full of sober thoughts, we lay down that night next to a bamboo grove we all remembered. I believe, trying to capture it now, that we heard voices, maybe even songs. I know we shivered and wakened and held onto each other. I think we smelled or felt fire, but safe fire. Maybe it was a dream.

The next morning when we went to the creek, besides drinking, we put water on our faces and skulls.

My daughter's lips started to quiver. I saw she was afraid, not for why you think! But because of how she thought we all might look.

I admit something of the same stirred in me; I thought

my heart might crack again, but my friend said, "Courage!"

Then the six of us began to joke. "You go first," we said to our neighbor. "You're the cutest."

"Yes, I am," he said. "I'm glad you noticed."

He folded his arms against his strange chest, the way Indians in the movies used to do. "Come on," he said. "Let's get it over with."

One by one we walked down the last defile. If there had been cars here, they had been pushed away. Our feet felt . . . asphalt, the asphalt of a real road.

Then we saw the Pacific, the peaceful ocean. I heard Denise behind me, starting to cry. "Oh, Mommy. Oh, my God." Skip stopped. He had more to remember than I did, lives upon lives.

That neighbor! He grunted, then he shouted, then he started to trot. We watched him gallop down across the Pacific Coast Highway. His body disappeared from view and came up again into our sight. There was something funny about the way he moved; he slipped and fell, and fell again, and half-rolling, half-walking, he tumbled into . . .

Into the long, low, slow, soft, rolling lines of blue and white surf. Heartstruck, caught between terror and joy, we watched his head, bright brown ball, rolling and tossing in the waves. He was swimming, waving, sputtering, skidding.

The real Beginning started for me. Because all I could see was a picture with my eyes, a cosmic frame; another world. Bright green hills on either side of us, and, of course, behind us, and on my right, as I looked toward the ocean, a low wooden building which used to be the Malibu Feed Bin but looked now more like the old *center* in the canyon, with four or five . . . *guys* lounging in front of it, and I thought I saw a woman and maybe even a *child* or two, just *doing business*, going about the chores of the day, as if this were the plain, the ordinary world. I saw in front of me the lush sweet thick blue ribbon of the sea, and above it the pale unscary band of sky, and even took in some *rubble* in the form of car skeletons and bleached-out two-by-fours and dying rubber tires. I heard voices in conversation, even calling out to us, but couldn't *pay attention* because the five of us were so worried, preoccupied, so locked in concern that that man who had put cobwebs on our heads when they were sore and bleeding, who had crept down his hill and crawled into our house when he thought he was going to die, but *he didn't die,* was maybe now going to (if we couldn't bring ourselves to "save" him), bite the big one, after all we'd been through.

"Richard!" Denise yelled. "Be careful, oh!"

Maybe *then* is when the Beginning started for me. Because into the frame came, you know what I'm going to say, a sail, and as its mast, a man. Well, it was wonderful to see, that wheeled board. And the brown feet that curled over it, held onto it, and the big brown body, that held out arms, that held the strong bright red cloth, and the rough voice that shouted out, "Hold on, Mate! We're coming for you!"

And as we moved closer down to the edge of the land, across the frightening highway (where there were people who drew back to look at us, and some turned away crying), the whole *beach* suddenly came alive with red and blue and pink sails and lifelines, and one man left his sail—which was neatly grabbed up by another—to dive into the water where he reached our Richard, whose laconic face was smitten with every kind of surprise, and with the aid of a . . . preserver, expertly thrown, pulled our neighbor out, and the six or seven competent and cheerful men pulled and hauled him over the several hundred feet of what used to be soft sand. Do you remember how *hard* it used to be, to walk across sand to the water? Do you remember sand between your toes, sand in buckets, on blankets, in your bathing suit? The dullness and softness of sand? The great heat of Beginning had transformed that sinking stuff, melting it into smooth jagged sheets of glittering colored glass that took the sun like rock candy, like lights in a jukebox, like jewelry in handfuls. It was that glass that Richard had slid down and was climbing back across now, helped by the lifeguards with their sturdy sails.

"Richard!" my little girl cried and dashed out onto the glacier surface to fling her arms about his neck. Her arms went about his neck and his great brown hands went to her breasts, covering her white star scars.

THAT NIGHT THEY PERSUADED US TO COME TO ONE OF THEIR small fires. To my surprise it fell to me to tell our story—the pane of window glass as it jerked from its precarious moorings in our old home on the skyline of Topanga, the last seconds before the thick air came to sear our skins and change it forever. How Richard came down to crawl in our house. How eleven of us slept in greying stiff sheets as the ashen air swirled around us for I didn't know how long, how my mother lived and died, how we walked the crescent, how we let the time pass, how fear came with the great plague. How we learned again to eat green things. How we began to talk and sing. To make jokes.

They sat close in and listened, and the light from the fire made them so beautiful. Then I told them how my heart split, and the terrible pain of it, as I remembered things that could be no more, and how my friend Skip had saved me with his courage and his patience, how I took all of it, all of that which could be no more, wrapped it in white light, coated it with pink, and sent all of it off in a bubble to become a star.

All of their faces obediently turned up to the dark blue universe as they searched for the star I told them about, and I saw peace come over their faces, but one old woman said into the dark, and the fire that had been tamed, "Surely, these are terrible times we have come upon."

But *I* was filled with a terrible rage and light, and I stood up and put out my arm to quiet her. *"No!"* I said. "Some people say these are bad times, but *I* say they are *good* times. We have bravery! We have love! We have the future. We have the Beginning! We have the present! Listen to *that* word, the Present. We all know what that is!"

And without thinking about it—how could I have *thought* about it!—I began giving her the fairly standard Lion Boyce zap II. The first was about money and the third was short and a little dispirited, but I always loved that second one so much that we'd stand sometimes in front of our California yellow refrigerator and just howl it out for the hell of it, but I said it now with conviction:

"Our universe is infinitely rich and exquisitely beautiful! We live in love, we live life fully and joyously! Our universe is dynamically aglow with Radiant Healing and Prospering Energy! We are aglow with Radiant Health!"

That one got a laugh, I can tell you!

"OOOO-Eee! It's good to be alive, and we ARE alive here in the heart of Infinity, here in our . . ."

I had never been much for talking. At least not in the past few years. But I had a vision of all I had to say to these people! How they must remember how to *cook*, how it had been so blindingly beautiful in those last weeks at Michael's. How they must never turn down love, because, outside of a wonderful meal, it was the BEST. How they should practice kindness. How they could move mountains! How beautiful they were now, how perfect in their competence.

Now I had very little hair on my head, but there was about a half-inch of it beginning to grow back, and it stood straight out. My arms crackled a bit, I could feel energy coming out of my fingers. I noticed in that second that my daughter had her face turned from me, buried in Richard's neck, and that

Skip was in his own world, his eyes turned inward. But I had so much to say. This fire! This blessed fire! Some say it was a bad thing, but I say it was a good thing! I waved my arms, and I could see radiant arcs in the sky, sparks from the jewels in my fingers flashing out into the night air. I caught the sharp smell of ozone.

"It's good to be alive and we ARE alive here in the heart of infinity, here in our infinitely rich, loving and beautiful universe!"

I saw it in their faces before I felt it. I loved it that they weren't afraid, that all I saw was curiosity and delight and a lovely *oooohh,* the acoustical equivalent of long low ocean waves breaking on glass. *Oooohh!* And I looked down to see the damp grass drying into a golden circle, two circles out from my thin, white-hot feet. I stood in a nest of electric smoke, clacked my hands together to see the sparks again.

I smiled, smiled so hard I thought the top half of my head might fly away.

Wow.

"Wow!" I said. "Some say it was the end, but I *know* it was the Beginning! Some will call this the Dark Ages, but I know this will be the Age of Light."

And the grass crackled under me.

"Hey, listen," I said. "No Biggie. I can remember years ago, when not a quarter of a mile from where we're sitting now, a girl used to study down in the Gulch . . ."

"I *told* you they used to call it the Gulch," a voice said in the semidarkness.

"And she had these faulty electric plugs, and one night she heard this awful thing and looked up to see this frog dancing on the wire."

"Radiantly *aglow,* no shit!"

And they got the giggles. Laughter rocked them.

"And then," I said, "she found out this man was being *unfaithful,* and she went out into the creek and caught a frog. She lined a box with greens and stuck the frog in and sent it to his office marked *This Side Up,* and he opened it.''

I sat down, and leaned forward a little, my arms in the air. I tried to remember what Lion used to say about creating a pyramid of light and putting everyone in it, keeping everyone safe.

"Now *that frog,*" I said, "that frog had been waiting in the post office for at least three days for the opportunity to jump. And when that man opened up that harmless little box . . .''

"He jumped!"

"That's *right.* He jumped so far, he jumped over the desk and the switchboard and the word processor and the *man* said . . .'' And they listened to the story and forgot everything else.

And that's how I knew that Lorna wasn't a quack and Lion wasn't a crook. That's how I knew the miracles they told us to expect had come. What a triumph, what a kick, what a beginning.

NOT THAT I DID THAT FIRE STUFF OFTEN. I DIDN'T WANT to and I didn't have to. They didn't need me. I just added to what they already had. But they did let me tell stories, in my turn. I use words that are pearls now, words, which—under heat—have melted from existence. I speak in a language no longer attached to what is real. How pretty those words were! *Hoodoo. Tarmac. Triscuit. Television.* I hope someday others will come to us, other people, other words, from the other side of the world. But if they don't that's OK. Jewels are beautiful before, during and after the time they are discovered. Our words, our lives, shine by themselves.

Here, in a short form, is what happened to the people along the beach.

Many people were killed south of Playa del Rey. Even now people don't go down there. And further inland, it was the charnel house that everybody had predicted. On the whole, they say, people got *what they expected*. The generals and the military were very hard hit. A certain kind of women and children were devastated. Fires destroyed the city and many died of thirst. The plague also raged for some months.

But, as in any catastrophe, there were the crackpots who hadn't paid much attention; the ones who, in a sense, went on playing poker through the quake. They were the dumb ones, the sissies, the . . . hedonists who were too enchanted by their own lives to get excited by Death descending. Of course they also included, sometimes, the dedicated survivalists, those who had toughed it out underground with guns and dried fruit, and who were rumored now to be engaged in vicious skirmishes, fighting over who would own the scorched, dangerous, inland earth.

But messengers have come to us, by foot and by boat, to say that people lived *all over,* in midwestern sod huts, and in Florida swamps, and especially in the great canyons of New York, where an entire cranky tribe survives underground, and the Dirty Dozens are their stories!

The ones I know who lived were the ones who had been making love, or napping, or fixing dinner, when the End came, or the ones at the beach—who still talked about the great crystallization of the sand, the ones far out windsurfing who dove beneath the waves and felt the whole Pacific turn lukewarm, the ones whose boats were out on the far side of Catalina when it came and hove to, sailing back out of pure curiosity. And, of course, all of the scrabbling canyon weirdos, who saw the whole global collapse as just another brush fire.

As I say, the ones who decided to come *west* instead of heading east, were by and large the ones who made it. And the wackos, the ones who used their belief systems, were the ones who got control over the radiation. Control is a silly word. It was surrender, really. The ones who *relinquished* control, who took it as it came, who seem— out here at least—to have lived.

Now some people have questioned me. How come *you* get to tell stories? And why should we believe *you* can make fire, and why should we believe *your* version?!

In answer I say first, if a Caspar can destroy a world, why is it so strange that an Edith should preserve it? And then I say, mine aren't the only stories! Just take a walk out on the glass.

All you'll *see* are the new people buttonholing each other (except there are no more buttons, buttonholes), telling *their* stories. Because those who lived, lived. And there are no more false prophets, only real ones. We're in the desert again, the New Jerusalem. So if you don't believe me, ask anyone around here.

We hear bad stories of a planned "invasion" from the inland, and sometimes we are beset by fear. But I remember that we too once "invaded," coming down from our mountain home, and how afraid we were. I know now that when ragged newcomers come down—scarred and sad—the sweetest thing we see is on their faces, when they look oceanward and see that some things haven't changed.

For the rest, we take it as it comes. We know there are things to worry about, but we are still in the grip of such relief and joy that we've come through—and we know death is so near to all of us—that we play the days away. We swim, and when the wind is right we lie in the sun; we weave baskets that aren't even *near* waterproof. When it rains we take shelter and doze. When the air is right and the stars shine we stay up all night and sing.

There's a woman about ten miles up the coast, they say, can work miracles and tell jokes. I wonder if it's Lorna. And little by little more old memories come back. I'll see a certain slumping little guy and rush up beside him to see if it's Hal, if he recognizes me, or I him. But what's to recognize? We've changed so much.

I should say that some girls have had some babies. Some babies are born angry or sad or marked, but mostly they're mellow.

When I say I tell stories, I mean, of course, I tell what it was like before, how there were maniacs abroad, and how heartbreak hurt the world, and some things were lost. But mostly I tell about *affirming:* "Everything always works out for us more exquisitely than we ever planned," or *Wu Wei;* practicing the wu wei shuffle—in fact we have a dance we do to that now, a very silly one. And we remember Norman somebody, and what he said about laughing, but I remember to tell that he was a man who believed in laughing, but who hardly ever laughed. That makes people laugh.

We sing. We sleep. Here's a story I tell, about the man who had ten thousand bees in a matchbox, and he was going to teach them to sing grand opera. Or have the Industrial Revolution. Or split the atom. Whatever. And so this guy tells a friend or a colleague or an enemy about his plans. (I draw this part out a lot. And they're all very good about laughing.) But then the friend says, *"Are you kidding?!?!* Ten thousand bees in a matchbox and *you're* going to teach them grand opera? Why you can't even, why, the difficulties are . . ."* (and people chime in with all the difficulties). So finally—you know the end of the story—the guy tosses the matchbox and says, "Fuck it, it was just a hobby." I've seen them laugh for an hour straight at that one. Then someone will call out, "Well, it's all in the telling!" And that will set them off again.

Half a life before, on an acid trip in the canyon, young-to-middle-aged divorced wife, I'd looked in the mirror and saw myself old. Saw my father's lust and my mother's fury. Saw past that to my own lust, fury, grudge-holding, saw past *that* to a human soul, nice, with six eyes.

Half a life later, one brackish, sweaty, hazy, California winter day, I wanted to wash my face and scraped away some foamy scum from a tide pool in Topanga Gulch. There I was, when the ripples stopped, toothless, almost gumless, not a hair by now to be seen on my billiard head, my lids growing back in a kind of bright yellow, my nose looking very unessential, like one good poke might knock it off for good and all. But I saw someone who had tried to love men and wasn't ashamed of it, who had kept the memory of her best friend forever, who had a grandchild for each knee, who wasn't scared anymore—or hardly ever—who could, if she had to, start a fire by heating up her fingers; above all, someone who could, by low means, or any means, make people smile, laugh, remember.

OOOO-eee.

There will be those who say it never happened, that we squeaked through. Believe them if you can.

There will be those who say that the end came, I mean the END, with an avenging God and the whole shebang. And many more who say it came, and there was death and terror and weeping in the streets, and the last man on earth died in the Appalachians, of pancreatic cancer, all alone. I *heard* that story, and I don't think much of it. You can believe what you want to, of course. But I say there was a race of hardy laughers, mystics, crazies, who knew their real homes, or who had been drawn to this gold coast for years, and they lived through the destroying light, and on, into Light ages.

You can believe who you want to. But I'm telling you, don't believe those other guys.

Believe me.

About the Author

Carolyn See is a book critic for the *Los Angeles Times* and lives in Topanga, California. She is the author of the highly acclaimed RHINE MAIDENS, THE REST IS DONE WITH MIRRORS and MOTHERS, DAUGHTERS. She also co-authored LOTUS LAND and 110 SHANGHAI ROAD, which were written under the *nom de plume* Monica Highland.